Grapefruit Beach

a novella

Eric Suhem

ISBN 978-0-359-21429-7

Part 1: Driftwood, Seaweed and Kelp

"Is that a grapefruit floating around in the kelp?" asked Alex. He was walking along the beach with his college roommate Omar, hours after they'd completed the semester's final exams.

"Either that or a cantaloupe," said Omar as the cold seawater bubbled around their toes. A wave quickly broke in, and the wayward citrus was washed away. "So you'll be starting that job on Monday?" Omar asked.

"Yeah, it'll help with the tuition," replied Alex. While drifting through his vague college curriculum, Alex had gotten a job as a computer operator at a construction company downtown.

"Is computer work something you want to do as a career?" asked Omar.

"I really don't know yet."

"Alex, you need to have more ambition and direction," said Omar, who was crunching spreadsheet numbers on the fast track toward a Business degree and lucrative connections in the corridors of power.

On Monday, Alex started the computer operations job at the construction firm. He worked on a team distributing print reports, loading disks on storage drives and monitoring computer system performance. Alex helped on day shifts and night shifts during the week and on weekends while also doing his college work. He often forgot to bring his security badge to work, which required him to obtain a temporary badge from the security guard, a burly woman named Dove, who sat at the front desk in the lobby, wearing the blue blazer of the security company. "Here's your badge," she intoned in a singsong voice that seemed to transform the lobby into a meadow, with birds fluttering around the fluorescent lighting and flowers growing out of the carpet. She would then return to speed reading one of the many paperback novels piled up at her desk.

Over a number of days they chatted, and Dove slowly invited Alex into her life. He visited her in an old purple Victorian house she shared with two other women in a bohemian neighborhood, enjoying shared herbal smoke on their back deck amidst exotic potted flora. Dove had a guitar, and she played songs while they sat in ramshackle chairs, viewing the colorful surrounding houses and yards. At other times, Alex sat behind Dove on the back seat of her motorcycle as she showed him neighborhoods he'd never seen, the city flying by in a blur of colorful lights. In Alex's mind, the black-and-white suburban world of his childhood receded, popping into a vibrant metropolitan collage.

Alex continued his work in computer operations, getting to know some of the others on his team. He noticed how happy many of the computer operators were, which may have been due to the copious amount of marijuana they inhaled. "Time for a smoke break," announced the lead operator. Alex followed him out the building, and they walked along the downtown pavement to an empty lot under the freeway overpass, where other office employees, many in business suits, were enjoying the benefits of ganja smoke. After regaling Alex with stories about his wild life, the lead operator said, "I need to go bail my brother out of jail. Can you cover for me in the computer room?"

"Sure," said Alex, inhaling some more smoke and then returning to work, enjoying the bending of reality as he loaded disk drives and printed computer reports.

Another computer operator was a part-time rock band bassist who had a variety of pills: uppers, downers, etc. "I've got anything you need, Alex," he said while removing vials of differently colored pills from his ubiquitous black leather jacket. For the most part, though, Alex abstained from the extracurricular chemical activity, applying himself diligently to the computer operations tasks while working toward a Computer Science degree at college.

"I'm trading my motorcycle for an old Toyota minivan," announced Dove to Alex one day in the construction firm's lobby. That night, after some more herbal tokes on the back deck, they rode across town on Dove's motorcycle to a dark, gothic apartment building on a garbage-strewn street. A dented, gold-colored Toyota van sat in front of the edifice, gleaming like a 14-carat jewel in a pool of sewage. "I'll name it Libre," said Dove as she gazed delightedly at the vehicle. Dove and Alex found the van's owner, and the transaction was completed, crumpled pieces of paper changing hands. "This van will take us on a voyage to new adventures!" enthused Dove.

The van seller's roommate, a German photographer named Ilse, was ensconced on a couch, perusing a large photo book of geese and ducks. "I'd like to join you on your journey," said Ilse, looking up from a grainy photograph of a mallard.

Dove and Alex talked with Ilse for a while, until Dove finally said, "Yes Ilse, come with us!" in a spirit of bonhomie.

Soon, Dove, Alex and Ilse were in the Toyota minivan heading back across town. Ilse aimed her camera lens out the smudged windows, snapping the shutter at the city's foggy streets. After a couple of miles, the van sputtered and slowed, finally stalling in a dark alley of broken streetlights and jagged, littered glass. A group of black-leather-clad bikers approached, their leader malevolently appraising the situation through demented eyes. "Engine trouble?" he asked, venom oozing into his voice as he thumped a large wrench in his palm.

Dove suddenly recognized him from her past, when she had worked as a counselor at a homeless shelter. It was a past that was largely mysterious to Alex. "Hey Spike, how are you doing? Staying off that crystal meth, I hope," she said.

"Well, I do what I can, Dove," said Spike, recognizing her as well, his mood lightening.

"Can you help us out here?" she asked.

"Yeah, let me take a look at it," said Spike. He quickly adjusted Libre's engine components with his wrench.

"We roam the streets, doing good deeds and helping those in need," said one of the other bikers, "excuse me for a minute." He hurried down the sidewalk to help an old woman cross the street.

Spike toiled on the engine, and after a few more minutes, the van was running again. "It was cosmically misaligned, but now it's in sync," he diagnosed helpfully. Dove, Alex and Ilse thanked the bikers and got back into the van, resuming their expedition.

Over the next few weeks, Dove, Ilse and Alex drove Libre around the city, exploring obscure avenues, the Toyota's engine purring efficiently, thanks to Spike's repairs. Turning down a side street, they encountered a lush green park with a lake surrounded by trees. "I never knew this was here," said Alex as they got out of the van and wandered through the greenery. Settling down on a swath of lawn, and indulging in some more herbal smoke, Dove told Alex about her plans to become a candle artist as Ilse looked on dispassionately, adjusting settings on her camera. "A candle artist?" asked Alex.

"Yes, creating colorful designs with melted candle wax," said Dove.

"I want to take a picture of that goose," uttered Ilse, enchanted by a gander that waddled toward the lake, where young children and old men operated small remote-controlled boats. Ilse pursued the goose determinedly, aiming her lens at the honking fowl.

"Let's go to the beach," announced Dove, and they were back inside of Libre, rumbling across town toward the ocean. The beach was nearly deserted when they arrived, a gray mist in the air. Dove and Ilse explored some tide pools in the rocks as Alex veered off toward a pile of driftwood and seaweed that had washed up onto the sand. He picked up some of the kelp and seaweed, arranging it abstractly, feeling unexpectedly filled with possibility, as if it was a portal to a wondrous new way of being. Alex had never felt this way before, and the images of the natural beach detritus would remain imprinted upon his mind.

The next day at the construction firm, the lead computer operator handed Alex a piece of paper with a number on it. "Get this tape from The Void," he said. Alex went down the hall to the tape library, where a large tranquil bald man named Lloyd sat on the floor, exuding the aura of an oracle, his posterior ensconced on colorful pillows, rolls of belly fat pressing up against his dress code-compliant button-down shirt. In between monitoring the locations of magnetic tape on the data shelves, he was reading a dusty tome containing obscure texts and unrecognizable symbols.

"Hi, Lloyd, where can I find this tape?" asked Alex, showing the tape number to the tape librarian, whom the operators referred to as The Void.

"Aisle 5, slot 162," said The Void in a voice laden with unknown significance. After Alex retrieved the tape, The Void handed him a grapefruit with an exclamation point printed on its skin.

"What's this for?" asked Alex.

"You'll need it for the future," said The Void mysteriously. He got up from the floor to check printouts detailing the tape library catalog. Alex went back to the computer room and gave the tape to the lead operator, who loaded it onto a tape drive for daily processing.

Visiting Dove at the purple Victorian enclave that night, Alex showed her the grapefruit that The Void had given him. "The tape librarian at work gave me this grapefruit. He said I'll need it for the future."

"Hmm…strange," commented Dove. She lit up a spliff and put on Brian Eno's 'Discreet Music', becoming immersed in the tonal subtleties of each sound. Alex then put on Bob Dylan's 'Subterranean Homesick Blues', one of many rock songs with lyrics that corresponded to his own questioning of what was considered a 'normal' path, the marijuana opening up his mind to alternative ways of looking at things. "20 years of schooling and they put you on the day shift, look out kid, they keep it all hid, better jump down a manhole, light yourself a candle," sang Dylan.

"Light yourself a candle…I like that line," said Dove. She found some cylindrical blocks of wax in a cupboard and set the wicks to flame. Later on, feeling hungry and laughing uncontrollably about the behavior of Dove's housemate's dog, they ate the grapefruit.

Dove, Alex and Ilse spent more days at the foggy coastline. At the end of one of those days, while holding Ilse's hand, Dove announced, "Ilse and I have decided to move south down the coast to a beach town. We'll be driving Libre there next week." Alex knew that Dove and Ilse had gradually become a couple, but he was surprised that they would be leaving town. "I believe in serendipity," said Dove, going on to describe how just when she'd found out that she and her housemates were being evicted from the purple Victorian, a friend of hers was going on an extended vacation to Tasmania, and had asked Dove to take care of his apartment at a place called Grapefruit Beach, rent-free, while he was gone. "Serendipity!" reiterated Dove.

"You should join us down there, Alex," said Ilse. She aimed her camera lens toward waves crashing against a seawall.

"I'd like to, but I'm too tied up with college and the job," said Alex, feeling a pang of regret as they got into Libre and headed back toward the city.

After Dove and Ilse moved south, Alex continued working in computer operations, completing the rest of his college courses in a haze of marijuana smoke and graduating with a Computer Science degree. Arriving for work at the computer room one day, he saw a supervisor from another department angrily berating one of the operators. "WHERE THE HELL IS THE BACKUP TAPE FOR THE MONTHLY INVENTORY REPORT!!?" screamed the supervisor, veins throbbing in his reddening forehead.

"You'll need to take that up with The Void," said Alex.

"The what?"

"Our tape librarian." Alex led the supervisor to the tape library, where The Void sat cross-legged on a colorful mat, incense filling the air.

"WHERE THE HELL'S MY TAPE!?" screamed the supervisor.

"Now, sir, just take a deep breath and relax, give yourself over to the philosophical concept of nothingness," said The Void.

"GODAMMIT JUST FIND THE TAPE!"

"Hey Alex, the manager wants to see you," said one of the computer operators, entering the tape library.

"Okay, I'll be right there," said Alex as The Void calmly looked for the supervisor's inventory backup tape in the library catalog.

"I'll take care of the tape, Alex," said The Void.

"Okay thanks, Lloyd." Alex went out the door and headed down the hallway to the manager's office.

"C'mon in, Alex, have a seat," said the data center manager, a rotund man nearing retirement. Alex entered the office and sat down as the manager absently scraped some crumbs on his desk into a geometric pattern. "Now Alex, you've been doing a great job here and you're a well-liked member of the team, but unfortunately, due to budget pressures, we will soon be outsourcing and dissolving the current computer operations staff. However, we have an opening that's come up at our programming compound in the desert. With your college work in computer science, we feel that you'd be an excellent candidate. It would be a great opportunity to eat, sleep and live 'programming' 24x7 while you potentially progress into new levels of responsibility. Of course, it would require you to relocate to our desert office."

"Sounds like quite an opportunity," said Alex.

"Think about it, and give me an answer by Friday."

"Okay, thank you, sir." Alex left the office and walked back down the hallway as the manager mulled over his retirement plan.

Alex passed by the tape library and looked in. The Void had retrieved the missing inventory backup tape, and the formerly angry supervisor was lying on an orange meditation mat in a sort of fetal position, hugging the tape closely. "I am going to give you a mantra of 'Butterfly', so whenever you feel stressed out, just repeat your mantra while visualizing butterflies fluttering in a field of flowers," said The Void.

"Ohhmm…" intoned the placated supervisor, sighing peacefully, closing his eyes.

Alex continued down the hallway back to the computer room, where news of the impending outsourcing hung over the operations staff like a dark cloud. "This company doesn't care about us, they just want to use us up. That's why I want to enjoy every day. Life's too short not to," said the lead operator. He prepared to go outside and smoke a joint under the freeway overpass with the other office workers.

"Yeah, I guess it is," said Alex while typing in data on a computer terminal's black screen, the small green digits shining brightly.

That night, Alex called Omar, his former roommate from college, and described his earlier meeting with the data center manager. "He said I could either move to a programming compound in the desert or get outsourced. If I do get outsourced, then I'm thinking of moving down south and living at the beach with my friends Dove and Ilse. What do you think I should do?"

"Well, of course, you should take the programming assignment in the desert compound. This is an opportunity to get your career started in programming," said Omar, who was in the process of accumulating capital for a startup venture.

Alex then called Dove at Grapefruit Beach. "It's beautiful down here, the waves are supreme! I'm learning to surf soon!

Ilse's being a bit difficult, pining for Berlin, but she'll adjust," said Dove. After the call, Alex thought some more about serendipity and the grapefruit that The Void had given him.

The next day, Alex turned down the desert programming opportunity and resigned his job. His manager, who had one foot out the door himself, didn't seem to be too upset about Alex's decision. "Between you and me, the desert programming compound sounds like a hellhole," said the manager, who had just returned from a 3-martini lunch. Eventually, the programmers in the desert would also be outsourced, the office space in the compound being liquidated and sold to a self-actualization cult. "Good luck to you, Alex," said the manager. He shook Alex's hand and returned to the golf resort and retirement pamphlets on his desk.

Alex said goodbye to the lead operator after sharing one more marijuana joint with him under the freeway overpass. "So what are you going to do after the outsourcing?" asked Alex.

"I'm going to enjoy every day of my existence here on planet Earth," said the lead operator with a smile. He inhaled another hit of smoke.

Within days, Alex packed all of his worldly possessions into his subcompact car and drove hundreds of miles down the coastal highway to Grapefruit Beach.

Upon arrival in the beach town, Alex noticed the swimmers and surfers walking around in the streets, seawater dripping from their hair in droplets on the pavement. Driving a couple of miles further, Alex arrived at an apartment building located footsteps from the ocean. The structure was decaying and rundown, covered with climbing twisting vines and surrounded by a teeming garden of ivy, lilacs, poppies, honeysuckle, rhododendrons, azaleas and hydrangeas. Purple, red and orange flowers bloomed amidst a chaotic tangle of vegetation. Alex got out of the car and wandered amidst the wild plants in the garden while inhaling the brisk sea air. His reverie was pierced by the sound of two voices involved in some sort of argument. Recognizing the voices as Dove's and Ilse's, Alex wound his way through the garden back to the apartment building where he saw the gold Toyota minivan Libre parked in the carport. Looking at the tenant list by the front door, Alex found the name Libre by apartment 3G and pushed its buzzer. Dove answered and buzzed him in. He climbed the stairs to their apartment.

"Alex you made it! C'mon in, we're just having lunch!" said Dove. She pointed to macaroni & cheese on the kitchen table.

"Hey Alex!" said Ilse, who was feeding a grapefruit into the grasping maw of a juicing contraption on the kitchen counter, steel blades slicing up the rind and pulp.

"This is the strangest place, grapefruit just kind of appear on the beach. We found this grapefruit earlier today by some tide pools," said Dove while pointing her spoon at the spherical tart fruit.

"Maybe a shipment of grapefruit fell off of a freighter and has been floating in with the tide," suggested Alex.

"I don't know, but it's very mysterious," said Dove while reaching for some macaroni & cheese. After lunch, she said to Alex, "You can sleep here on the floor, we have lots of room." Alex unpacked his sleeping bag and laid it on the floor near a pile of paperback novels that Dove had been speed reading.

"Hey the waves look great, let's go bodysurfing," said Alex, looking forward to diving into the ocean.

"You go ahead, Ilse and I are embroiled in some drama right now, we'll see you later," said Dove. She went into the bedroom with Ilse and closed the door. As Dove and Ilse shouted angrily at each other from behind the door, Alex changed into his swimsuit and walked out to the beach. A number of people were in the ocean on a sunny day, enjoying the waves. As he floated in the water, Alex thought about how much his life had changed in the past 24 hours. He did not know where it would lead, but he was open to whatever would happen. He caught a wave and rode it in, feeling an instant vibe of freedom.

“I want to learn to surf, and the apartment manager said he’d loan me one of his surfboards,” announced Dove the next day. She and Alex went downstairs to see the manager, a surfer named Lunski.

“Yeah, this board is good,” mumbled Lunski while staring for a long time at a surfboard with a grapefruit decal on it. There was a chess board set up on Lunski’s kitchen table, and a couple of cats slept on surfboards along the floor. Alex peered through a doorway into one of the rooms in Lunski’s apartment, where he saw a thick granular carpet of sand covering the floor, making the room effectively a large sandbox. “I like the sensation of the beach at all times, even when I’m indoors,” explained Lunski. “Here, take this too,” he said, handing a boogie board to Alex as Dove picked up one of the cats, a big ball of fur.

“Thanks a lot, hey that looks like an interesting book,” said Alex. He pointed at a book of cosmically cryptic symbols similar to what The Void had been reading in the tape library at the construction company where Alex had previously worked. Dove petted the cat and then set it back down on the floor.

“Oh, it’s just some light summertime reading,” cackled Lunski insanely.

“Okay Lunski, well thanks again,” said Dove as they left the apartment. Lunski’s cats walked over to the apartment’s adjacent room with the sand-covered floor and did what cats like to do in piles of sand.

As Dove and Alex were obtaining the surfboard, Ilse was downtown, taking photographs of people at a bus station near skid row, hoping to capture “the gritty essence of the American underbelly”. Hours later, she returned from her downtown photography expedition. “I walked along the cracked sun-bleached sidewalks near the bus station, taking photographs of hardened working-class men, focusing on the deeply-etched lines in their faces as they stood in the bleak sunshine, waiting for a bus. Then I saw geese and ducks wandering on the sidewalk among some derelicts. I got some good pictures of mallards on skid row.”

“Ilse, Lunski just loaned me his surfboard, and I’m going to take a surf lesson tomorrow. I want you to be my ‘Betty’,” said Dove.

"Your what?"

"My 'Betty'. That's the surfer's girlfriend, who sits on the beach being supportive."

"I don't want to have anything to do with surfing culture. I see surfing as an apocalyptic venture festering at the edge of the American continent," said Ilse.

"WHY DO YOU HAVE TO BE THIS WAY?" demanded Dove angrily, and the two women repaired to the bedroom to continue their arguments. Alex quickly changed into his swimsuit and took the Lunski boogie board out to the ocean, where he enjoyed numerous wave rides.

When Alex returned to the apartment, Dove and Ilse were still arguing. "Should I come back later?" asked Alex.

"She's out of control with her madness!" said Dove dramatically while gathering her guitar and some cannabis, "let's go!" Dove and Alex got into the gold Toyota minivan Libre and motored along the coastal highway as the sun was setting. They parked the van near a darkening beach, got out, and walked along the sand, feeling the kelp and seawater between their toes as Dove played the guitar. Finding some driftwood that was strewn amidst the waves, Alex created an impromptu sculpture, stacking driftwood and rocks with strands of seaweed in a sort of unconscious exhilaration. "I hear a drum," said Dove as they walked further along the beach in the moonlight.

Over the next sand dune, they found a group of people in a drum circle surrounding a bonfire. "Hey Dove!" they called, as she seemed to know everybody. Dove and Alex joined the drum circle and soon they were all dancing under the stars. Dove picked up her guitar and started singing songs that she'd written, mesmerizing the crowd with her powerful, melodic voice. Afterward, Dove and Alex returned to Libre for the drive back home to Grapefruit Beach.

Upon arrival at the apartment, Dove and Ilse closed the bedroom door and launched into a new round of loud conflict. After about an hour, Ilse emerged from the bedroom with her bags packed. "I'm moving back to Berlin, can you drive me to the airport, Alex?" she asked. Dove wordlessly stalked out of the apartment and strode toward the beach.

Soon Alex and Ilse were in his car, headed to the airport. "It just didn't work out between Dove and me. She and I are going in different directions," Ilse said while examining one of her camera lenses.

"Yeah, I noticed you two were arguing a lot, but I was hoping you'd work it out. I'm really going to miss you, Ilse."

"Well, you should come and visit me if you ever find yourself in Berlin." She gave Alex her address in Germany.

After dropping Ilse off at the airport, Alex thought about his living situation. Dove had invited some friends from the drum circle to move into the apartment, and he wanted to find his own place. An unemployed surfer had recently been evicted from an apartment down the hall, so there was a vacancy. The next day, Alex talked to Lunski, who said, "Yeah man, you can have the apartment, I just need first and last month's rent." Alex dipped into his savings to pay the rent and deposit amounts but knew he'd have to find employment soon. He began a job search using his sparse computer operations resume, pounding the pavement and contacting various employment agencies, eventually finding work with a software distribution firm called TechniSel.

"Welcome to the team, you'll be working on the night shift," said Alex's new supervisor Pam, a short, prim, efficient woman in a gray skirt and horn-rimmed glasses. "You'll be teamed with Jerome, our graveyard shift lead operator."

That night, Alex showed up for work at 11:30 p.m. and punched in his time card. He used his security badge to enter the computer room and walked along the large white tiles to the console area, where he found a large bearded man sprawled out on a chair. "Hi, I'm the new computer operator," said Alex.

"Hey man, I'm Jerome," said the lead operator, rising from his chair to shake Alex's hand. Jerome went over the basics of the job with Alex: mounting tapes and disks on media drives, retrieving printouts, uploading and downloading files, running jobs that executed computer programs, basically the same as Alex's previous computer operations job at the construction firm. While showing Alex how to reset a communication line, Jerome said with serious conviction, "A few days ago, I took some LSD and then stared at some ants on my back porch for 3 hours, admiring their teamwork and camaraderie, there's a lot we can learn from them."

"They are industrious little guys," agreed Alex.

On Alex's second night at TechniSel, the job training continued. Toward the end of the shift, when the work slowed, Alex and Jerome played backgammon. Alex talked about his beach-influenced view of life, and how the driftwood, seaweed and kelp were finding a foothold in his consciousness.

"Yeah man, the beach speaks to me too, the ocean waves crashing at the end of the continent are good for the soul," said Jerome.

The computer room phone rang with an angry user on the line, screaming about his morning inventory report. Alex handled the problem and more calls. When the night shift ended at 8 a.m., Pam entered the computer room with a stack of forms. "We have a new problem reporting system," she announced to Jerome and Alex, "I want you to fill out a service request for each issue encountered last night so that we can better monitor problem resolution."

“I have to go drive my kid to school, can you take care of these?” whispered Jerome to Alex.

“Sure, I’ll do it.”

“Thanks, man.”

Alex spent the next 3 hours filling out the forms to Pam’s exacting specifications. “It’s important that we maximize the efficiency of our processes,” said Pam in a businesslike manner as she clicked her ballpoint pen repeatedly. After completing the task, Alex returned home in the morning sun, stopping at a diner for breakfast.

On Alex’s third night at TechniSel, he showed up for work and got the turnover from the swing shift operator Troy, who had a side business doing electrolysis. Troy gave Alex one of his business cards depicting a needle-shaped electrode applying an electric current to destroy hair roots. After Troy left, Alex and Jerome initiated some data downloads and monitored batch jobs. Suddenly one of the air conditioning units in the computer room malfunctioned, creating strange noises. “Did you hear that? There are ghosts in the machine!” blurted Jerome, white powder lurking under his nose, his eyes darting around amidst the air conditioning units. He ran to a computer screen and started typing frantically on the keyboard. “Yes, here it is, ghost in the machine: a phrase used to highlight the perceived absurdity of mind-body dualist systems where mental activity carries on in parallel to physical action, but where their means of interaction are unknown, or at best speculative!” he declared triumphantly.

“Jerome, there’s an error light warning on one of the air conditioning units. I’ll need to call the repairman,” said Alex.

“Okay man, I trust you, it looks like you have a good grasp on things,” said Jerome, running out to his car in the parking lot, where he spent most of the shift in a paranoid state of mind. He returned to the computer room at 6 a.m., just before Pam arrived at the parking lot in her Toyota.

On Alex’s fourth night at TechniSel, after completing most of the tasks for the shift, Jerome said to Alex, “Would you mind covering things? I need to take a nap.” Alex knew that Jerome also worked a full-time job during the day, so was often half asleep during the night shift.

"Sure, no problem," said Alex.

"Thanks, man," said Jerome. He proceeded out of the computer room to the adjoining office area, where he laid down on a printout distribution table. "It's good for my back," he said when Alex asked why he preferred to sleep on the table.

A couple of hours later, as the sun was coming up, Alex returned to the office area where Jerome was snoring amidst the printouts. "Hey Jerome, you'd better get up, the managers are coming in soon."

"Yeah man, okay." Jerome raised his head from the 'Quality Control Report', which he was using as a pillow.

They went back into the computer room, and Pam arrived for work a few minutes later, noticing the disheveled reports on the table. "This table looks like somebody's slept on it," said Pam. A few hours after that, Pam typed up a memo reiterating the need to keep the printout table neat and organized. "The printout tables should not be used for purposes other than distributing reports," emphasized Pam in the memo.

As Pam was sending out the memo, her phone rang. "Pam, would you join us in the conference room, we need to discuss task reassignment," said the I.T. department manager on the other end of the line. Pam hurried to the conference room, where a number of executives and managers were in the midst of a meeting. Taking a seat at the conference table, she noticed tarantulas crawling around in the corner of the room on the gray synthetic functional carpeting. A whiteboard was covered by praying mantises, and locusts had taken over an empty ergonomically-compliant swivel chair. "As you can see, Pam, we're having a bit of an insect infestation problem. It's a long story concerning a disgruntled entomology data expert who unleashed these bugs on us after we fired him," said the I.T. department manager while crushing some crawling beetles with his coffee mug. "We could bring in a professional exterminator, but for budgetary and publicity reasons, we'd rather keep this in-house." He pulled a large white exterminator suit out from under the table, along with a sprayer and tanks of bug spray. "We'd like you to take care of this, Pam, as you've displayed an excellent aptitude for multitasking, and no promises, but a promotion may be in the offing for you." He handed her the exterminator suit, and she looked at the other managers at the conference table, all men with expectant looks on their faces, the boys' club in full force.

"Yes, sir," said Pam in a businesslike manner, showing that she was up to the task.

On Alex's fifth night at TechniSel, he punched his time card, walked into the computer room and got the shift turnover from Troy. "Uh, I had a phone emergency with one of my electrolysis customers, so I didn't really have time to run the backups, and the batch jobs haven't been completed, and the printouts need to be distributed. Also, Jerome called in sick, and Pam is here working late."

"Yeah, okay, I'll take care of it."

"Thanks, Alex," said Troy as he left the computer room.

A few minutes later, Pam walked in, wearing the big white exterminator suit. "Your initial progress review is coming up, so I need to observe your work," she said briskly. For the next hour, Alex handled an unusually hectic workload of urgent user calls, printout distribution, and hardware outages while Pam sprayed bug killer in the back of the room on the large white tiles near the air conditioning units. She also managed to observe Alex's work performance and scribbled copious notes on a clipboard. "Okay, my assessment is complete, thank you Alex. Troy is waiting out in the office area, I'll be giving him his performance review next." She clicked off her ballpoint pen and left the computer room.

After printing some more reports, Alex took them around to different distribution destinations within the building. One of the things that Alex liked about working the late shift was wandering the empty building at night, absorbing the peaceful stillness, feeling enveloped in a meditative calm.

On the other side of the building though, unbeknownst to Alex, the quiet was being shattered by increasingly intense moans in the executive office print distribution area. "Give it to me some more!" growled a woman's voice. The voice belonged to Pam, prone on the printout table, having shed the white exterminator suit, the computer operator Troy atop, straddling her. "That's it, that's right!" moaned Pam throatily, her horn-rimmed glasses tumbling to the gray functional office carpeting.

"Quiet Pam, someone might hear us!" urged Troy nervously.

"Just do your job, lunkhead," said Pam. She became lost in thought, drifting into a dreamlike vision of… *a train barreling down the tracks of a mountain railroad through a foggy twilight, entering a tunnel. Though the train was charging through the dark passage, somehow the tunnel still seemed empty. Pam was the only passenger on the train, which pulled up at an underground station. A grapefruit rolled down the aisle of the passenger car and out the train's doors, into the darkened station, which was illuminated by only a few flickering light bulbs overhead. Pam followed the grapefruit toward a door covered with dark green moss and tangled vines. The door opened into a well-lit room and the grapefruit rotated inside, followed by Pam, who then found herself standing before a long desk of insect-headed administrators clad in black business suits. The administrators passed files of papers back and forth as the grapefruit rolled around on the floor near Pam's feet. A grasshopper passed a file to a praying mantis on its left. The praying mantis looked at the file and then loosened its black tie, announcing, "Case #547, Pam Snaff, Technical Supervisor." The praying mantis stared at Pam and then addressed her, "Pam, you're attempting to thrive in a professional world dominated by men. You'll need to be hard as nails, work 3 times as much as the men, and in our eyes, it still won't be enough!" Pam noticed some tanks of bug killer with a sprayer in a dim corner of the room and she moved toward the insecticide. As she drew closer to the bug spray, fully intending to use it on the administrators, tarantulas moved quickly along the floor and stopped in front of the bug spray tanks, impeding her path. "This little movement toward the insecticide will be going on your record, Pam," said the praying mantis disappointedly. The green triangular-headed insect imprinted a red-inked stamp on Pam's file and then started laughing uncontrollably. Pam just stared at the administrators as the grapefruit rolled out the door and back into the train station. The tarantulas herded Pam out of the room and back onto the train, which quickly left the station and emerged into the bright morning sunlight. She sat alone in the passenger car as the sun shone on the car's green vinyl seats...* Suddenly Pam snapped out of it and found herself back on the printer table outside the TechniSel vice president's office, still consuming Troy's rhythmic thrusts. "You know, Pam, I could schedule an electrolysis appointment for you to remove some of this unwanted arm hair," grunted Troy, ever the electrolysis professional, noticing the stubble near Pam's elbows. He then pulled out and ejaculated, drips of semen landing on one of the desk's computer reports.

"Did you just cum on the executives' inventory report?" demanded Pam, back in business mode. She put on her horn-rimmed glasses to examine the milky smudges that obscured numbers on the report output. "Make sure this gets reprinted before the executives arrive in the morning!" she ordered. They put their clothes back on, and Pam headed out to the dark parking lot, where she got into her Toyota and headed home.

A few days later, Dove and Alex were walking in the sand along Grapefruit Beach. "I've found a job as an assistant for the performance artist R.," said Dove.

"Isn't R. the one who reads monologues in candlelight with a rat on her head?" asked Alex. He vaguely recalled seeing a picture of R. in an alternative weekly magazine, walking through a garbage dump with a rodent clinging to her scalp.

"Yes, she emphasizes animal rights in her performances, and among other things, I'll be responsible for maintaining the candlelight ambiance while she's on stage."

"Well that should tie in with your explorations of candle art," said Alex as he took another hit of sinsemilla. Dove had begun creating candle art, melting wax into collages, and was looking to make connections with the downtown artistic community.

"Why don't you join me at the afterparty this Friday night?" she suggested before inhaling a lungful of herbal smoke.

"That sounds good, maybe I'll meet some artists interested in driftwood sculpture," said Alex.

That Friday, Alex and Dove went to R.'s show in a small downtown performance space. Alex sat in the sparse audience while Dove monitored and lit candles at the side of the stage. R. recited stark and provocative monologues about environmental degradation and economic imbalance while performing a sort of experimental dance with a still and well-behaved rat on her head. Any slight movements of the rat would alter the performance in unpredictable directions. As R. elucidated in her Artist's Statement: "Rats have a lot to teach the human race, which is why I keep one in close proximity to my brain during a performance."

After the presentation, Dove introduced Alex to R. "R., this is my friend Alex, he's into driftwood sculpture," said Dove.

"Oh really," said R. dismissively as she turned her attention to a minion dressed in black. "Tanya, gather the group together, we need to find more rats."

In a few minutes, Alex was out in a back alley with R., Dove, and the rest of R.'s team, searching for rats. "We think of them as 'found objects'," said Tanya.

"I hope this rat isn't diseased," said one of the minions while grasping for a biting rodent in a pile of garbage.

“This is the afterparty?” asked Alex.

“I see the search for rats as part of the process of the performance,” said R. as her smartphone rang. “Excuse me a moment, I need to take this call....Yes, mother...No mother...Yes, I’ll buy some Kleenex on my way home...Well, why is the ironing board not folding up correctly, did you push that little latch underneath?”

“So what do you do, Alex?” asked Tanya.

“I’m a friend of Dove’s, just here in support. I work as a computer operator at TechniSel.”

“Oh that’s interesting,” said Tanya, losing interest in the conversation.

“I’m also getting into creating sculptures out of driftwood, seaweed and kelp,” added Alex.

“I just wouldn’t be able to work for a corporation, I’d feel like a dehumanized robot, working for The Man,” said Tanya.

“We are artists! We’re following our true passion, we don’t sell out, and we’re not ‘corporate whores’, no offense,” said another minion walking alongside them, his hand clutching a paper bag containing a found rat.

“Well I’m sure a lot of people who do art do other stuff on the side to pay the bills, not necessarily defining themselves with one rigid identity,” responded Alex. The minions shrugged, and continued their search for rats. Alex looked at his watch and saw that his work shift would be starting in about an hour, at midnight. He said goodnight to Dove, who would get a ride home from the minions. Alex got into his car and headed to work.

Arriving at TechniSel, Alex looked forward to a night of working with data, the logic and orderliness helping him to feel centered and grounded. At times he felt drawn to wandering a windy beach, encountering chaotic clumps of driftwood, seaweed and kelp, then perhaps forming the detritus into some sort of intuitive sculpture, no plan in mind. At other times, he craved the structure and sequential organization of information technology. This was one of those times. He arrived at the computer room and ran the nightly batch jobs which executed programmers' code. If a job terminated abnormally, Alex would have to contact the after-hours on-call programmer, who would log in from home to try and fix the problem. In extreme cases, the on-call programmer would have to drive into work to correct the program. As Alex was resetting some of the network communication equipment, a beep went off from the main console, indicating that one of the batch programs had failed. He checked the on-call list and dialed the programmer Bill Pleck's number. A woman answered groggily, "Hello?"

"Hello Mrs. Pleck, this is Alex from the TechniSel computer room, could I please speak to Bill?"

"It's 2:15 a.m.! You people called us last night! Why don't you leave us alone?!"

"I'm sorry, it's just that Bill is the on-call programmer, and…"

Bill Pleck eventually got on the phone, and Alex described the problem. "Uh….okay I'll take a look at it," said Bill Pleck. Alex then heard a *clunk*, as Bill Pleck dropped the phone and started snoring.

"Hello? Hello?" said Alex.

As time went by, Alex continued to do his job steadily, moving up the ranks from computer operations to operations analysis, switching from the night shift to the day shift. Alex was assigned to share a cubicle with the programmer Bill Pleck. Although Bill Pleck had fallen asleep on the phone that one night, he was the fulcrum on which the entire department depended, smoothly solving multiple programming issues daily. "Bill Pleck is the unsung hero of the programming team! Without him this company would go under!" declared one of the other software engineers.

After working with him for a couple of weeks, Alex marveled at how Bill Pleck was able to multitask so effectively, calmly keeping his head while others around him were losing theirs. "One needs to mentally become a machine," advised Bill Pleck. When rumors spread about an impending reorg and possible layoffs, Bill Pleck was a rock of unruffled assurance. "They'll never get rid of any of us, we're too important to this company," he said unworriedly in his mellifluous dulcet tone.

The next morning, Pam announced, "There's going to be a meeting today in about an hour. You're all required to attend."

During the meeting, the programmers and computer operations staff learned that there would be a restructuring of the Information Technology department, centered on 'outsourcing solutions'. "Our new team members will consist of interns from nearby universities, and a service bureau located in Tasmania. In order for you to receive your severance packages, you will need to train your replacements for a period of 3 months," said the I.T. department manager, a large, intense man with great ambitions.

Alex was sitting next to Bill Pleck, who had been humming peacefully but now jolted upright and started screaming, "WHAT??!! I GAVE THIS PLACE THE BEST YEARS OF MY LIFE!! I HAVE A FAMILY TO SUPPORT! DO YOU KNOW HOW MANY TIMES I HAD TO GET UP IN THE MIDDLE OF THE NIGHT TO FIX EMERGENCIES AND SAVE A LOT OF CUSTOMER ACCOUNTS FOR THIS COMPANY?!"

"We appreciate your service, and you will be compensated accordingly after you complete the 3 months of training your replacement," said the I.T. department manager while leaving the conference room with the other managers, who were patting each other on the back.

Bill Pleck screamed and rushed at the managers, waving his arms frantically in the air, brandishing a stapler. A security guard who had been placed in the conference room for just such an occurrence rushed forward and tackled Bill Pleck, just as the stapler was inches away from the I.T. department manager's skull. "AAGGH!! AAGGH!!" yelled Bill Pleck as another security guard found some Ethernet cables on the floor and used them to wrap up the screaming software engineer in a sort of makeshift straitjacket.

Jerome was in the back of the conference room and Alex walked over to him. "I don't understand it, Bill always seemed so together," said Alex.

"It's all part of the complex tapestry that is Bill Pleck," said Jerome while the software engineer was being hauled away, his screams filling the hallway. Alex felt relieved that he had kept a certain emotional distance from his job as he and Jerome looked out the window at a raving Bill Pleck being shoved into a white van, headed to the Information Technology Home for the Criminally Insane.

Alex showed up for work the next morning and learned that Jerome had been fired. "During the night shift, he went to sleep in the vice president's chair and was snoring there when the vice president arrived in the morning," said Pam. "Alex, we're going to need you to go back on the night shift and fill in temporarily to help train Jerome's replacement."

That night, Alex showed up for the graveyard shift and Pam was there with a college intern. "Alex, this is Leo, he's very bright and he'll be taking over for Jerome as part of the department's restructuring initiative."

Over the next few nights, Alex showed Leo the tasks of the job: loading tapes, printing reports, running and monitoring the batch jobs, cleaning and maintaining the peripheral equipment, problem reporting escalation procedures. "This'll be easy, but I'm not finding anything about this when I check online on my phone," said Leo.

"Most of this is not online, you just need to learn by doing it," said Alex.

"Oh, I see," said Leo doubtfully. The next night, as the computer room's phone started ringing nonstop with calls from the Tasmanian service bureau, Leo packed his things and walked out the door into the night, never to return.

Alex continued to work the night shift as Pam and management resumed a hiring search for Jerome's replacement. After a few weeks, Alex was curious about how Bill Pleck's recovery was progressing, so one morning he decided to go downtown and walk up the long flight of cement steps to the Information Technology Home for the Criminally Insane, a towering gray edifice atop a hill.

In the cavernous lobby, Alex was met by a nurse in a starched white uniform. She wore orthopedic shoes and had a permanent leering grin, possibly a result of plastic surgery gone awry. "Can I help you?" asked the nurse.

"I'd like to see Bill Pleck," said Alex.

"Oh yes, this is a big day for Mr. Pleck," said the nurse, "he'll be undergoing conversion treatment."

The heels of Alex's shoes echoed loudly on the floor as he was led down a bleak corridor by the nurse, insane laughs and screams emanating from behind each locked door. At the end of the corridor, a janitor ran a floor buffer in continuous circles. "Mr. Pleck is in here," announced the nurse when they arrived at a cell midway through the hall.

Alex went inside the cell, where sitting in the corner was a fetal-positioned lump wrapped in a straitjacket. "Bill, is that you?"

The crumpled form stirred on the floor and looked up. "Alex, long time no see!" declared Bill Pleck suddenly, bounding up to his feet. They talked for an hour and Alex was impressed by how lucid Bill Pleck was, seeming just like his normal old self. "I've even been writing programs here at the asylum," said Bill Pleck. He showed Alex some of the computer code he'd written on napkins and scraps of paper.

"Bill, I always wondered why you snapped like that at TechniSel, you were always so even-keel."

"Well Alex, I was sitting in that outsourcing announcement meeting, thinking 'okay I'll just find another job' when suddenly out of nowhere, a grapefruit appeared in my lap, screaming that I was nothing unless I excelled at my job. It's true, I crave approval from the job to fill the emptiness inside. I just started going insane staring at that screaming grapefruit pulp. After that, I have no memory of what happened." Bill Pleck looked at the shadows cast on the cell floor by the window bars. "But, they've tuned up my drug regimen and I'm making rapid progress in my rehabilitation. They're going to give me some electroshock volts today, so I should soon be right as rain, ready to rejoin the workforce!"

"Well that's great, Bill," said Alex as white-suited attendants entered the cell and wheeled Bill Pleck off to the electroshock room.

When Alex got back to Grapefruit Beach, the first thing that he noticed was that Dove's Toyota minivan was covered with flower stickers, looking like either a hippie cliché or a colorful plastic shower curtain. Dove said that she'd been reading a book called 'The Sunlight-Filled Life' and was inspired to put flowers on Libre to attract and reflect more of the positive energy of the universe. "I want to live in the light," she said, going on to describe a desire to transcend her past, which she cryptically labeled as a 'murky corridor of abuse'. Looking at the flower-covered Libre, Dove said to Alex, "It's a beautiful day, let's go for a picnic."

They packed a lunch and headed out on the coast highway, turning inland for a few miles, and eventually parking near a bucolic flower-filled meadow. The only other vehicle in the parking lot was a truck labeled 'Have a Nice Day Charities'. There were large 'Have a Nice Day' smiley faces brightly painted on the side of the truck. Dove and Alex got out of Libre and wandered amidst sunflowers, daisies and butterflies. After finding a picnic spot and leisurely eating lunch, they lied down in the grass and stared up at the clouds. Dove fell asleep and floated off into a dream....*in which she decided that her Toyota minivan needed to be washed. She drove Libre along a street, and made a right turn into the "Lil' Ferret Car Wash", maneuvering Libre through the lot, past some colorful plastic pennants flapping in the wind. Coming to a stop, she was met by the attendant, a short man dressed in a brown furry costume with a rubber ferret mask. "Good morning, ma'am, will your minivan be having the 'Basic', the 'Plus', or the 'Deluxe' wash today?" asked the attendant.*

"Deluxe," said Dove without hesitation.

"Of course," said the attendant. The car wash was the kind in which the vehicle is aligned onto a metal track and slowly propelled through a gauntlet of rotating brushes and undulating flaps of soapy rubber. "Now please just drive your minivan onto the 'Cleanse-Track' and we'll do the rest." Dove maneuvered Libre onto the track, ready to be pulled into the car wash when she saw the attendant frantically knocking on her window, his furry brown costume becoming somewhat matted by water spraying out of the car wash. Dove rolled down the window and the attendant breathlessly said, "Would you like a complimentary

snack from our car wash kitchen? It will provide nourishment and sustenance on your journey through our cleansing tunnel." He presented some grapefruit chunks on a plastic plate. "The only thing on the menu is grapefruit," said the attendant, his eyes peering out from inside of the hot rubber ferret mask. Dove took the plastic plate of grapefruit chunks and closed the window as the mechanism of the car wash lurched into motion, conveying Libre forward toward the spinning brushes. Dove ate a few grapefruit chunks while staring out the windshield at the spray of the car wash's water jets. "The brushes will scrub right down to the nub of your soul!" called the attendant ferret, looking distorted through the suds on the window.

Becoming mesmerized by the rotating brushes, Dove blinked her eyes in the dream and suddenly found herself no longer inside Libre, but instead in a black Rolls-Royce Phantom Coupe, speeding along an endless dark highway at night. White dash lines in the middle of the road flew by as raindrops thumped loudly on the coupe's roof. Dove pressed the brake pedal and tried turning the steering wheel but it had no effect, the car propelling forward of its own accord. One of the side windows of the Rolls was church-like stained glass, and it depicted a traumatic moment from Dove's childhood, a night when a 'friend' of the family held her down in a broom closet and burnt her skin with a Bic lighter and hot dripping candle wax.

Suddenly appearing next to her in the front seat of the Rolls was the little car wash attendant in his brown ferret costume, the suds-soaked fur a little bit worse for wear. "You must stay on the road, drive into your past, collide head-on with these formative traumas!" urged the car wash attendant. Dove looked through the windshield, the childhood scenes from the stained glass windows slowly appearing on the black highway in front of her. "You must confront who did this to you, and bring closure!" persisted the ferret-masked car wash attendant. The Rolls was speeding forward when a 20-foot high grapefruit appeared in the middle of the highway, and there was a jagged CRASH.....

Dove's dream suddenly jolted to the parking lot near the meadow, where she and Alex had just left Libre for their picnic. Her golden Toyota minivan was engulfed in flames. "LIBRE!! HOLY %$#^&!!" screamed Dove. The 'Have a Nice Day

Charities' truck had crashed into Libre, an explosion ensuing, the driver of the truck staggering around the parking lot and then lurching off into the nearby shrubbery. "LIBRE..." cried Dove as she stared at Libre's flower stickers and the truck's 'Have a Nice Day' smiley faces melting in the inferno...

Alex shook Dove awake on the picnic blanket. "Dove wake up! You were having a bad dream!"

"WHERE'S LIBRE!?" she shouted. They ran back to the parking area, finding Libre where they had left it, shining brightly as if it had just been through a car wash. The 'Have a Nice Day Charities' truck was also still in the parking lot, the driver taking a nap. "This is a sign from the universe," said Dove while clutching her worn copy of 'The Sunlight-Filled Life'. They walked over to Libre and got in. Dove turned the ignition key and took a deep breath. "Let's go," she said.

Over the next few days, Dove thought more about her dream of the car wash, the Rolls-Royce and the ferret. She decided to leave Grapefruit Beach and return to the Midwestern place of her childhood to confront her disturbing past. The day before she planned to leave, Dove and Alex took a walk on the beach. It was cold and windy, waves crashing on rocks as they moved through the sand. When the sun had set, Dove launched into a soliloquy about a woman who was wandering through an enchanted forest on a path illuminated by moonlight. Along the woman's way, she encountered rocks and trees, each of which was inhabited by some kind of spirit. Dove seemed to be possessed as the words emerged from her mouth for about 20 minutes, describing in great detail the woman turning into a princess, magically recreating herself and going off on a journey while emitting a sparkly green light.

After Dove finished her speech, Alex stared at her, and then they hugged for a long time. Alex was once again stunned by how brilliantly creative her mind was, but it wasn't the kind of mind suited to the world of careers and paid employment. No longer working for R., Dove was struggling through a series of menial jobs. He thought about how her sensitivity and imagination were not valued by society, diminished by shallow people whom she had to serve in the world of commerce. After walking further down the beach, Dove and Alex hugged again, happy that their souls had encountered each other.

"I've always seen something in you, some sort of inner electricity, just follow that, along with the driftwood, seaweed and kelp," said Dove, her countenance lit by the dim glow of the moon.

The next morning, Alex woke up to find that Dove was gone. "Yeah, she packed up that gold Toyota van in the middle of the night and just drove off," said Lunski while sanding down one of his surfboards. "I looked out the window and saw her driving away, with some sort of sparkly green dust coming from the van's exhaust pipe." Alex thought about Dove's story of the princess exuding magical green light as she walked down an enchanted path.

He drove into TechniSel, where it was his last day of work. Alex exchanged farewells and goodbyes with other outsourced co-workers who, like him, were there to collect their severance pay after completing the 3 months of training their replacements. Pam and the I.T. department manager were busy devising staffing solutions for further outsourcing plans, ignoring him as he walked out the door. While driving back to Grapefruit Beach, Alex looked at his severance check and decided to spend it on a trip to Europe, where he would experience the driftwood, seaweed and kelp on foreign beaches. He also wanted to visit Ilse in Berlin. A couple of days later, Alex bought a ticket for a plane flight overseas.

Arriving in Europe, Alex explored scenic beaches, where he built impromptu sculptures of driftwood, kelp and seaweed. He bought LSD from somebody on the street in Amsterdam and tripped out while looking at the wooden buildings and canals of the city, along with the vibrant colors of the paintings in the Van Gogh museum. Visiting a beach in Brighton, on the southern coast of England, he walked in the sand, picking up rocks to which he was spiritually drawn, hearing Dove's voice saying, "There's a living soul in everything, even these stones." Alex saw teeming life in the driftwood, seaweed and kelp along the shore. He was also surprised to see not grapefruit, but rather nectarines and apricots washing up on the beach.

Alex contacted Ilse when he arrived in Berlin, learning that she had become a successful photographer who had a solo show coming up at an art gallery. "The last I remember, you were including ducks and geese in photographs of city scenes," he said while drinking coffee with Ilse at a café near her apartment.

"Yes, I've combined it all into a comprehensive point-of-view, incorporating poultry into gritty street settings, here's my portfolio." Alex looked at pictures of fowl in squalid urban milieus. "It's about the intersection of desiccated man-made structures with nature, discussing man's impact to the environment," said Ilse. Alex examined further samples from Ilse's portfolio: one was a photograph of a chicken pecking at spectacles on a window sill, another was a photo of geese surrounding a radiator in a rundown flat. "A critic in a weekly alternative newspaper has attacked my work as being rife with clichés, but he's not understanding it. I'm satirizing the clichés that are prevalent in popular culture," said Ilse. She took a sip of coffee. "So are you still making driftwood sculptures, Alex?"

"Yeah, I'm incorporating rocks into it too, I found some good misshapen stones in Brighton when I was traveling through England."

"Alex, for my upcoming gallery show, I want to include a 3-dimensional sculptural component. I think driftwood, seaweed and kelp would add an interesting counterpoint to my photographs. Would you like to collaborate with me on this?"

It didn't take Alex more than 2 seconds to think about his response. "Yes, Ilse, that would be fantastic!"

Over the next couple of weeks, Alex worked with Ilse and her team, preparing for the gallery show. Ilse's main assistant was a woman named Oona, who fluttered about the studio in a smock and bright pastel pants, talking about anything off the top of her head. "The lemurs dance to the off-key music of the universe, so it's important to understand the symbolic significance of what the duck quacks," advised Oona as Alex was busy attaching a crucial piece of seaweed to his sculpture.

"Oona, could you hand me the glue?" asked Alex. In response, Oona did a pirouette and danced out of the room, inadvertently knocking a can of blue paint onto the floor, the dye streaming along the floorboards.

"Oona is important to the creative process," insisted Ilse, deciding that the patterns of spilled blue paint would be an essential addition to one of her photographs depicting a goose maneuvering through a slum alley. Alex could feel an impulse rising within him, perhaps influenced by his information technology days, in which he wanted things to be concrete and on-schedule instead of floating off into a vague utopian cloud of non-achievable goals, but he just shrugged his shoulders and the work continued.

On the day of the art show, Ilse and Alex shared thoughts about the work with the gallery visitors. Oona saw a duck on the sidewalk and left the gallery to pursue the wayward fowl, never returning until the next day. The response to the art show was decidedly mixed. One blogger pointed out that Ilse's photographs were "pointlessly strange beyond comprehension," adding, "I don't see the point of it!"

However, there were also some positive responses. "This photograph provides a fresh take on well-mined tropes of suburban ennui," said a critic from a weekly newspaper when analyzing Ilse's picture of an empty, cracked backyard swimming pool that had geese walking around in the deep end. The critic went on to say that Alex's inclusion of driftwood and kelp in the swimming pool added an intriguing naturalistic aspect.

Afterward, as they sipped wine from little plastic glasses, Ilse said to Alex, "I don't know what's going to become of this, but when I'm really old, I think I'll look back on this time and really value it. Some people consider my work odd and strange, but it's what I'm believing in right now, and I think I'll be glad to have been so crazy in my time."

"Yeah, we should take advantage of a creative impulse when it's there because it can just desert us at any time," said Alex.

Later that night, Ilse went to sleep and started to dream......*she was walking through a mansion in which each wall, the furniture, everything, was electric blue. Within the bright blue milieu, geese and ducks wandered around, honking and quacking. As always, Ilse was ready with a camera, and she eagerly snapped photos of the fowl in the electric blue setting. Going down a flight of stairs, she discovered an underground indoor swimming pool. The pool's underwater lights shone through the rippling water, casting swirling shadows on the pool area's cement walls. In the pool were mallards, and Ilse took pictures of them too.*

*Then suddenly, Ilse was outside of the mansion in a garden of crawling vines, stone sphinxes and statues. Butterflies fluttered through the air and a grapefruit rolled around in the garden's vegetation. She picked up a cracked hand mirror from the ground and looked into it. Her face was now wrinkled with lines, seeming to have aged decades. She thought back to earlier when she had excitedly photographed mallards in the subterranean indoor swimming pool. Now she couldn't imagine why she would have wanted to do such a thing. She reviewed those photographs on her digital camera, finding that they had all turned black. All she wanted to do now was sit on a stone bench in the garden and stare at the statues and sphinxes.....*Ilse awoke with a start from the dream, knowing that she had to get started on her next project as soon as possible because, as Alex said, the inspiration could leave at any time.

A couple of days later, Ilse, Alex and Oona were sitting at Ilse's kitchen table, drinking coffee and eating grapefruit. Ilse was planning her next creative venture. "I'm thinking about making photographs that juxtapose rodents with the electronic boats that we used to see in the lake at the park. It's going to speak of mobility and transience. Also, Oona will be having a greater influence on this project, I like her artistic vision."

"Chaos is mandatory!" decreed Oona, scooping pulp out of her grapefruit and throwing it against the wall.

"So Alex, I'd like to include some of your kelp conglomerations in this new project," continued Ilse, "would you like to stay here and work with me on this?"

Alex sliced his grapefruit in half and looked at it, feeling himself split between either staying to work on Ilse's art project, or going back home to work in I.T. Alex didn't feel as if he fit in to a definite identity as either an information technology professional, like some of the people he'd worked with, or as an artist, like Ilse. He just saw himself as a human being doing those different things. Oona threw another grapefruit half against the wall. Its acidic juice and pulp dripped down the wall's chipped beige paint. "Thanks, Ilse, but my money's running low, and I should probably be headed back to the states," said Alex.

After breakfast, Alex wandered around the apartment, happening upon photographs Ilse had taken of Dove in the past. "No half stepping!" Dove had admonished Alex many times before when he'd tried to split his time between information technology and driftwood sculpture. He looked at Ilse's photographs: some with Dove in the nude on a tenement roof, waving white scarves around in a dramatic way, others with Dove sitting alone in a street gutter with her head down. "That's how I'll remember her," said Ilse.

Alex bade farewell to Ilse and bought a plane ticket, returning home. Resettling at the beach, he needed to find a job. Not seeing any economic opportunities in driftwood sculpture, he cobbled his resume together and returned to information technology, finding work at a data company called InfoGrab.

On Alex's first day there, his team lead, a woman named Cindy, approached his cubicle. "I've got assignments for you already!" enthused Cindy while placing program service requests on his desk. "I just **love** computer code! It **excites** me!" she squealed after having been up all night programming, though she had managed to take a short nap between 2 and 3 a.m. During the nap, Cindy had a dream about computer code punctuation and woke up exhilarated. "I saw in my dream that I needed to use a comma instead of a semi-colon on line 1793 of the subroutine!" she declared excitedly.

Cindy then took Alex to see the managers of the department. "We have multiple layers of management here, but the two managers to whom we report directly are Don and Ed," said Cindy while leading Alex to Don's office. Don was an ex-Marine who had been in the data processing industry for over 30 years. "This is a great place to work, isn't it Don!" gushed Cindy.

"Better than a kick in the teeth," said Don.

In the next office was the other manager Ed, who was wearing a polyester retro disco shirt that clung to his pot belly. "This is Alex, the newest member of our team," announced Cindy.

"Alex, I think you'll find that working here is better than a poke in the eye with a sharp stick," said Ed.

"It's sink or swim here!" effervesced Cindy, her voice rising to one big exclamation point.

After a few weeks on the job, Alex settled into the team's workflow. He got his latest assignment from Cindy and walked back to his cubicle, seeing a woman walking down the aisle to the empty cubicle next to his. She was wearing a long flowing colorful print dress and exotic steel jewelry. "Hi, I'm Julia, the new programmer," she said to Alex while removing small wooden statuettes from a bag and placing them on her desk next to the keyboard and stapler.

“Hi Julia, I’m Alex,” he said while observing the miniature obelisks she was lining up near her tape dispenser, “what are those?”

“I use these to remind me of who I am and to stay grounded, otherwise my head goes flying off into the clouds,” said Julia. She then attached some small mandalas to her cubicle wall.

Cindy walked over to Julia’s cubicle. “Welcome to the team, Julia, I see you’ve met Alex. You’re our two newbies!” She put a programming assignment on Julia’s desk, knocking over a miniature totem that Julia had carefully placed near her printer tray. Julia frowned at the toppled figurine.

“She seems insane to me,” said Julia to Alex in the lunch room a couple of days later, discussing Cindy, who was in her cubicle squealing with delight over debugging a program. “She acts so nice and cheery with an aura of daffodils and butterflies, but there’s a dark disturbing vibe there. Also, why is she always carrying that stuffed animal around?” Julia was referring to the little pink unicorn Cindy often clutched while berating other programmers for poor coding practices.

“Well yeah, Cindy’s kind of intense, but I think she’s basically a fair person. She just gets a little wound up about software development, and seems to take any perceived lack of job commitment as a personal affront,” said Alex while buying some potato chips from a vending machine. “Hopefully you’ll be able to put up with her calls in the middle of the night,” he added, noting that he had already endured a number of nocturnal phone communications from Cindy suggesting improvements in program code.

“Well, I’m not going to let her ruin my meditative calm,” said Julia. She took a deep breath and briefly gazed upon a ‘lunar Celtic priestess’ amulet that she extracted from her purse.

That night at 2 a.m., Julia was lying in bed when her phone rang. “Hello Julia, this is Cindy! I’ve just been going over some of your computer code, and I see a better way that it can be structured. Let’s go over it in the morning!”

“Uh…okay Cindy,” murmured Julia, half asleep.

The next night, Julia was sleeping soundly when the phone rang again. “Hello Julia, this is Cindy! I see where the comments in your code can be improved! Let's review it in the morning! Just trying to help!"

"Couldn't this call have waited for tomorrow, when we're in the office?" asked Julia groggily.

"Oh, okay, if you feel that way," said Cindy in a tone that seemed to question Julia's commitment.

"That woman keeps calling in the middle of the night with nitpicking suggestions!" complained Julia to Alex in the lunchroom the next day.

"Yeah, she does that, but management is on her side," said Alex while microwaving some sort of pocket sandwich. As they talked, Cindy walked down a hallway on the other side of the building to the 'Nap Room', a cell designated for brief employee dozing during the day. Naps improved overall productivity, and Cindy had been up working hard for the past 36 hours, helping upper management meet its revenue goals, so she thought it might be useful to take a 23-minute snooze. Clutching her favorite stuffed animal, the pink unicorn named Mr. Uni, she plopped down in one of the puffy bean-bag chairs that lined the floor of the room, and instantly dozed off into a dream….*in an empty house on a humid tropical island, Cindy scrubbed floors late into the night as large women in dresses with colorful floral patterns beat her with bamboo sticks. "Faster, faster!" yelled the large women, increasing the rapidity of the caning. Cindy scrubbed faster as exotic jungle creatures chirped outside. Finally, the women shouted, "Enough! You're useless! Out with you!" They cast her out of the empty house, with nothing but a compass and Mr. Uni, her little pink stuffed unicorn.*

Cindy looked at the compass, which displayed a poisonous flower instead of directional coordinates. She threw the compass into the surrounding jungle and moved through the tangled mass of dark vegetation, holding her pink stuffed unicorn. Hours passed by and she grew hungry. Around her were grapefruit trees growing incongruously in the humid jungle. She pulled a grapefruit from a slithering tree vine and carved it open, finding a key nestled within the pulp and rind. While chewing on the grapefruit, Cindy moved further through the undergrowth, suddenly encountering a bright red door embedded in a large rock amidst a dense snarl of vines. "Maybe this key will fit in the door, Mr. Uni!" she said to her stuffed animal. She inserted the key and it fit perfectly, the door opening into an elevator. Cindy boarded the elevator and looked at the buttons, which were tiny grapefruits with numbers printed upon them. Cindy pressed grapefruit #3 and the elevator began to descend. The number lights above the elevator door flashed in a random haphazard pattern: 4, 1, 6, 5, 2...

*Finally, the 3 flashed and the elevator arrived, the doors opening into a clean white pristine data center, where well-dressed professionals busily milled about in the service of information technology. Cindy looked out one of the windows, seeing that she was in a crisp white building situated in a yellowish green field amidst rolling hills. Other square black and white buildings sparsely dotted the landscape. She saw a profound beauty in how the precise sharp-angled black and white buildings were embedded into the natural terrain. Feeling refreshed by the air conditioning, Cindy walked into a cubicle that had her name on it. The walls of the cubicle were covered with smiley-face stickers. She sat down and looked at a computer console screen, seeing a programming assignment, and her heart lightened. She felt grounded and centered, knowing that she needed to completely give herself over to computer code and pour her identity into it. Cindy started typing on the keyboard, pushing images from the past out of her mind, the coding solutions coming to her instinctively, and she knew this was where she was meant to be...*Cindy's smartphone alarm went off and her 23-minute nap was over. With a smile, she rose from the bean-bag chair and got back to work.

Later that afternoon, Don, Ed and a couple of other managers were walking down the cubicle hallway when they passed by Julia's cubicle, now adorned with numerous mandalas tacked on the corkboard walls. Obelisks, mysterious statuettes and totems formed a sort of altar on Julia's desk. "What the hell is all this? Explain yourself!" demanded Don.

"I meditate upon these objects to center myself, and clear my mind so that I'm more in tune with the universe," replied Julia.

Don just shook his head and said, "California has nothing but fruits and nuts. I used to work in Texas, but that was all steers and queers." Ed laughed and they continued down the hallway, telling homophobic jokes. Julia took a minute to meditate while clutching an amulet in her fist, and then returned to working on her program. Alex, in the next cubicle, was tuned out, listening to music on his earphones while debugging a program loop.

"HA-HA-HA!" brayed Don and Ed as they walked past more cubicles, telling more homophobic jokes.

A voice rose from one of the cubicles. "Are you in repressed denial about your own sexuality, Don? Is that why you're so homophobic?"

Don turned around, trying to ascertain where the voice came from. "Who said that? Explain yourself!" demanded Don.

"I'll explain myself," said the voice, coming from a rotund programmer named Morris, who stood up in his cubicle. "I am gay, Don, and this is perhaps the 659th homophobic joke I've overheard from you in the three years I've been working here. If you don't stop, I'm going to go to HR and file a complaint against you."

"Look, just get back to work. I'm sorry if you're choosing to be offended," said Don, who then mumbled to Ed, "whatever happened to the good old days, when we could tell all the fag jokes that we wanted to, without all this 'political correctness'? Whatever happened to family values?"

"Yeah, you've got to watch your step these days, with all these metrosexuals running around," said Ed.

Don walked into his office with Ed and then called Cindy on the phone. "Cindy, do you have time for a little chat?"

"Yes Don, be right there!" chirped Cindy.

When Cindy entered the office, Don and Ed were discussing an organizational chart. "The culture of our group is very important, and we need employees who fit in. People should feel comfortable together and be able to tell jokes without fear of reprisal," said Don.

"We need to get rid of the misfits, without looking like we're violating discrimination laws," added Ed bluntly.

"Now this programmer Morris, I don't think he's contributing as much as he could be," said Don. He stared at the organizational chart and shook his head doubtfully.

"Morris has actually done a lot of good work, but Roland, on the other hand, is not pulling his weight. I'm becoming disappointed in his work ethic," said Cindy, referring to a middle-aged programmer who was out on medical leave.

"Yes, how much longer is he going to be in the hospital for those cancer treatments?" asked Ed impatiently.

"We do have a number of software engineers in their mid-50's I'd like to get rid of, but when we do so, we can't make it look like ageism," said Don while peering at the list of employees. "What about Julia?" he asked, "that woman gives me the creeps. Whenever I pass her in the hallway, it feels like she's glaring directly into my soul. And that Alex, I don't know if he's gay, but I do think he's some sort of deviant, spacing out and staring at those pictures of driftwood, seaweed and kelp in his cubicle."

"Both of them are doing good programming work," said Cindy in their defense.

"Well, let's keep an eye on them," said Don.

"It's how they can relate and be comfortable with each other. It brings them together," said Julia about the homophobia that pervaded the office. "If you don't laugh at Don's bigoted jokes, then they'll label you as 'not fitting in', and they'll find a way to get rid of you."

"Yeah, I'd guess that Morris has a target on his back now. I don't know why some people are so uptight about homosexuality," said Alex. He and Julia were in the lunch room, buying snacks from a vending machine.

"I've always subscribed to the theory that everybody is just somewhere on the sliding scale of sexuality, in between totally gay and totally straight," said Julia as she retrieved some potato chips from the machine's dispensing bin. "We find it easier to categorize than to look at shades of gray and try more to understand somebody as an individual," she added.

"Yes that's true," said Alex. He put some money into the coin slot of the vending machine. "Goddammit! It's stuck again," he said as a bag of Cheetos got lodged on the dispensing hook. Alex tipped the vending machine back and forth, trying to loosen the Cheetos from the hook.

That night, Don got home from work and was greeted by his wife. "How was work?" she asked, giving him a peck on the cheek.

"Well I had to be 'the bad guy' again, making staffing decisions for possible layoffs," said Don.

"They don't understand what pressure you're under from upper management," said his wife sympathetically. "The 'Have a Nice Day Charities' people called, another one of their trucks crashed and caught on fire, they'll need some help this weekend with their fundraiser."

"I'll be there," said Don dependably.

"That's my Don," said his wife. She gave him another peck on the cheek.

They had dinner, and a few hours later Don informed her that he was going to bed. "I have an early morning tomorrow," he said.

"Okay goodnight dear," she said, "I'll be working on this jigsaw puzzle a bit longer."

Don looked at the puzzle pieces on the table, partially forming a picture of a large grapefruit. "Looks like you're making some good progress on the pulp," he said.

"Thanks, dear, I'll be working on the rind next," said his wife as she searched through the puzzle pieces. Don went to bed and he thought about his goals for the next day, chief among them being the firing of Morris and Roland. Soon he was fast asleep and dreaming.....*Don sat on a hot white rock by a swimming pool, viewing bodybuilders in tight speedo swimsuits lying down near the water. He stared at their sweating muscular limbs spread languorously across the poolside furniture. "You are filled with vibrating waves of conflicted energy! Explain yourself, Don!" said the plump programmer Morris, who was swimming the backstroke in the pool. Soon all the bodybuilders in speedos were lined up in front of Don, their tumescent bulges insinuating themselves upon his vision. Licking his lips, Don leaned forward and pulled down the speedo of one of the bodybuilders, finding a hard and firm... grapefruit.*

Don woke up in terror. "Godammit, those queers have infiltrated my dreams too!" he muttered. Don looked to his wife in the bed for reassurance, but she was asleep and snoring, some sort of green cream beauty mask smeared on her face. Don became more determined to fire Morris.

The next day, Don called Morris into his office. "Morris, as you probably know from our disappointing quarterly earnings report, we are facing budgetary pressures that require some difficult staffing decisions. I'll just get right to the point. We're going to have to let you go. You have one hour to pack up and exit the building."

Morris directed a bitter smile toward Don. "So Don, you're trying to get rid of anyone who reminds you of your conflicted sexuality? Well, you people can't do this, you'll be hearing from my lawyer!"

"Yeah good luck with that, Tinker Bell, we've legally crossed all our t's and dotted all of our i's," said the other manager Ed, who was sitting in the corner of the room. Morris began to feel dizzy when looking at Ed's polyester shirt, which had a sort of swirling op-art pattern of black and white squares.

"Morris, if it makes you feel any better, we're also laying off Roland. Ed, I need you to go over to the cancer ward at City Hospital and give Roland his termination notice."

"Glad to," said Ed, "it will be good to get rid of some of the deadwood, ha-ha."

Morris just shook his head and got up to leave.

"Morris and Roland are no longer part of the team, they just didn't fit in," said Don as he addressed the programming staff an hour after the firings.

Alex and Julia looked at each other and then returned to their cubicles as Cindy approached. "We have a big project that's due in a week, and I'll be relying on my two newbies to pick up the slack and complete some critical sections of code!" She distributed new program assignments to Alex and Julia.

A little later in the lunchroom, as he was heating popcorn in the microwave, Alex said to Julia, "More layoffs and the work is being dumped on us."

"Well, in between Don's anti-gay slurs, Cindy's squeals of delight and Ed's undefinable evil, the three of them have been very effective in reducing staff to help upper management meet its revenue goals, and in the process, increasing their own bonuses," said Julia. She opened up her purse and placed a steel pentacle, a frayed picture of a black sun, and an 'evil eye' talisman next to the non-dairy coffee creamer and sugar packets on the kitchen counter.

"What are you going to do with those?" asked Alex.

"I'm picking up some extremely bad vibrations from management, and if they cross me, I will utilize the occult and deal with them in the unseen world," Julia said ominously.

"I've always pictured you as being more of a vessel for positive energy," said Alex.

Julia poured diet cola into a Styrofoam cup. "I have a dark side too, it's not all sunshine mandalas and lollipops," she said.

As the week went by, Alex and Julia worked hard on their programs, finishing on Friday afternoon, an hour before the deadline. "Whew…it's good to have that program done," said Alex, "you going to relax this weekend?"

"Yes, I'm going to let go of the stress," said Julia while arranging amulets on her desk. "How about you?"

"There's some new driftwood, seaweed and kelp that's washed up on the beach. I want to make a sculpture out of it." Alex then went home as Julia stayed to finish up some emails.

The manager Ed passed by Julia's cubicle and looked at the pentacle, black sun, and 'evil eye' items near her keyboard. "I dabble a bit in the occult myself, Julia," he said with a leer. "Did you know that the black sun is based on a sun wheel mosaic incorporated into a castle floor during the Nazi era?" Julia was unable to respond to his question, falling under the spell of the shining whirling pattern of black and white squares on Ed's garish polyester shirt. He noticed that she was beginning to drift off. "Get back to work!" Ed barked, returning to his office.

Opening a large gray steel file cabinet in his office, Ed searched through the 'G' section and found a file bulging with photographs. He placed the file on his desk and opened it, removing a picture of a large round grapefruit. Staring at the citrus, Ed thought dreamily about when he'd started his career. Back then, 'G' would have stood for 'Good Guy', because that's what Ed was, his co-workers calling him 'Good Ol' Ed'. Ed was full of hope and optimism in those days, brimming with kindness and an infectious smile. Every morning his wife would pack a lunch for him and give him a kiss. "Have a nice day, honey," she said, as their children gathered around.

"Bye daddy," they said, on their way out the door themselves, headed to school.

"Bye kids, be good," said Ed, playfully tousling their hair before leaving for work.

Over years of constant day-to-day adjustment to various cutthroat business environments though, Ed's outer veneer of cheerful optimism had been eaten away by a darkness that always lurked within, yearning for expression. Slowly, Ed morphed into a sadistic creature of the corporation, rationalizing his behavior by the fact that he had a wife and kids to support. "It's 'Eat or be eaten'," Ed liked to say, and he'd developed a voracious appetite for the souls of others. He learned to enjoy expressing his evil core at the office, and his escalating positions of authority gave him increased opportunity to maliciously control the actions of his subordinates. Ed looked one more time at the grapefruit photo and then put it back into the file, getting ready to go home for the weekend and enjoy time with his family.

On Sunday morning, Julia sat in bed listening to the birds sing. She stared at the sunlight cast upon the green plaster wall in her room and took a deep breath, letting go of all the negative energy from her job. Julia lived in a small studio apartment on the coast, about 10 miles north of Grapefruit Beach, and could hear the waves crashing outside. She felt the cool sea air from the open window, the thin curtains billowing in the breeze. She brought a mug of tea to her lips and took a sip. That was when the phone rang. "Hello Julia, this is Cindy! One of the testers found some issues in the implementation of our team's programs, and I'm going to need the entire team at the office today to fix this because as you know, our deadline is Monday morning. It will be all hands on deck!"

"Okay Cindy, I'll be there within an hour," sighed Julia.

"I'll bring some cookies and juice, it'll be fun!" enthused Cindy.

When Julia arrived at the office, the other programmers, including Alex, were already there. "Cindy's working with the testers, trying to analyze our team's block of code," said Alex while reviewing his portion for any errors.

Cindy was getting more excited as the work increased, pulling her pink stuffed unicorn Mr. Uni from her desk drawer for support. "Julia, could you come here please?" Cindy asked, looking as if she'd been affronted personally, her tone sugar-coated with malice. Julia walked over to Cindy's desk. "Now Julia, I don't want to point any fingers, but it looks like it might be a problem with your input loop procedure. I worked very hard on making our programs perfect, so I hope that your code hasn't messed that up! I don't want this to make me....I mean, the team...look bad!"

They pored over the program code for the next 2 hours, until the tester Len said, "I may have found something...uh-oh I might have been using the wrong input file..." He changed the input file and reran the rests, all the programs completing without error. "Sorry, my bad," said Len.

"No problem, Len, it helps us to beef up our error-handling," said Cindy good-naturedly. "Okay everybody, I guess you can go home. Oh Julia, do you have a minute?" As Alex and the rest of the programmers left, Julia returned to Cindy's desk. "Julia, it looks like your code was not the cause of the problem, but I see a number of areas that can be improved in your program. For instance, I think we could significantly expand the indentation and your use of comments. So if you could get that done by tonight's deadline, I think we'll be all set. I'm going home for dinner, but I'll be back later to check on your progress."

The rest of the programmers went home and Julia sat down at her desk to implement the changes in her program that Cindy had mandated. It was late Sunday and the office building was deserted, except for the security guard reading a horror novel at the front desk. A grapefruit suddenly appeared next to Julia's mousepad, startling her. Julia thought about cutting open the grapefruit and having it for dinner, along with a candy bar from the vending machine and some lukewarm slightly carbonated cola from the soda machine. But instead, staring at the round tart fruit, Julia drifted off into a dream…*she was on a gray platform under a mushroom cloud sky. Next to her was the manager Ed, in his customary retro disco polyester shirt, sweat stains spreading from his underarms. Farther down the platform was Cindy, busily typing on a keyboard. "Julia, you need to be more like Cindy," said Ed. "We take her intense need for approval, based on an emotionally turbulent childhood, and utilize it, making her a productive tool for InfoGrab. Oh Cindy, would you please stop typing, and devote the next 5 minutes to disfiguring this stuffed animal? You remember Mr. Uni, don't you, Cindy? You held him close when you were a child back on the islands, being forced to scrub the floors while the large women beat you with bamboo sticks." Ed walked over to Cindy and handed her a cuddly pink stuffed unicorn, along with a set of pliers. Small tears welled up in Cindy's eyes. She grasped the stuffed unicorn's legs with the pliers and began twisting.*

"Why is she doing that?" asked Julia.

"The point is that she's doing it efficiently, not asking 'why'. The company will reward her with the praise and approval that she craves. As for you, Julia, you're out of your league with your little pentacles and amulets, dabbling in the occult, meddling where you don't belong." Ed grabbed the pliers from Cindy and moved ominously toward Julia. There were screams from torture

*devices farther down the platform, and...*Julia snapped out of her dream and was back at her desk. She looked at the grapefruit and started to scream, "NO!...NO!..." finally stopping when the security guard ran over from the lobby.

"What's all that screaming, is everything all right?" asked the security guard.

"NO, EVERYTHING IS NOT ALL RIGHT!" Julia cleared her desk of the New Age trinkets and miniature obelisks, packing them in a cardboard box. She then stalked out the front door, into the night. "I'VE HAD IT! I'M NEVER COMING BACK!"

And she never did.

When Alex arrived for work the next morning, his phone rang as he looked at Julia's empty cubicle. "I'VE QUIT!" declared Julia on the other end of the phone line. "Unfortunately, I'm being evicted from my apartment. Do you know of anything available for rent?"

"Well, there's an apartment that freed up in the building I live in at Grapefruit Beach," said Alex, referring to the apartment that Dove had recently vacated.

"Grapefruit Beach, hmm, I've always noticed an interesting energy about that place," said Julia. Alex soon introduced Julia to the apartment manager Lunski, and a week later she moved into the building. Julia was enamored with the location, steps away from the beach, the air filled with the flowery scents of climbing bougainvillea vines, hanging wisteria, azaleas and lilies.

Julia spent hours wandering along Grapefruit Beach wondering what to do with her life. She found grapefruit lurking in all sorts of unlikely places: tide pools, clumps of ice plant, small caves.

One stormy day, she looked up at a sand dune and saw a lone stark figure on crutches, silhouetted against the sky. It was her neighbor Lars, who lived down the hall in apartment 3C. They had met briefly when she was moving in. With great dexterity, he was propelling himself on his crutches while also manipulating a metal detector along the sand's surface. He waved to her with one of his crutches, and she ascended the sand dune. Julia noticed that he was wearing a postal service uniform, including a regulation mail carrier bag. "Hey Julia, how's the apartment?" asked Lars.

"It's wonderful, I've been feeling a lightening of my soul since I've moved here."

"This beach is spiritually rich," said Lars as his metal detector beeped continuously, locating doubloons and gold pieces within the sand. "I put positive energy out into the universe, and it's returned to me in abundance." He put a number of found coins into his mail sack.

"Yeah, I can dig that," smiled Julia as Lars burrowed more coins out of the ground. "What happened to your leg?" she asked.

"Well one day on my route, I was delivering mail to a small nondescript house when I noticed rustling curtains in one of the windows. Suddenly, the house's front door burst open and a business of ferrets streamed out, heading straight for me. I tried to get away but tripped on a lawn sprinkler and fractured my ankle, falling forward and impaling myself on the yard's white picket fence as the ferrets tore at my leg. Somehow I managed to escape the yard and was able to hop onto a passing ice cream truck, leaving the ferrets squeaking viciously on the sidewalk. The first thing I noticed on the ice cream truck was that all of the popsicles were grapefruit-flavored. I turned toward the driver and saw that it was a mannequin dressed in a clean starched white uniform. The truck delivered me here to Grapefruit Beach and I moved into one of the vacant apartments. I'm quitting the post office, and am going to support myself with the rare coins I've been finding on the beach." The metal detector beeped again and Lars unearthed a doubloon. He placed it in his mailbag. "It would all be for the best, I didn't fit in at the post office anyway."

"It looks like you've found your true calling," said Julia, adding, "I'm still trying to figure out what mine is."

"You just need to look inward and follow your real voice," said Lars optimistically. He pressed the metal detector into the grains of sand.

Julia thanked him and suggested that they get together for dinner some time. "That sounds great," said Lars, "how about tonight at 7 p.m.? I'll be cooking a grapefruit soufflé in my apartment."

"Sounds good, see you then," said Julia. She descended the sand dune and continued along the beach.

At 7 p.m., Julia knocked on the door of apartment 3C, and Lars opened the door. "Julia, welcome! Come on in!"

She entered the apartment and instantly noticed that the entire floor was covered by an inches-thick layer of mail: letters, postcards, advertising flyers and more. "What's all this?" asked Julia, reminded of the sand-covered floor in Lunski's apartment.

"Just some perks of being a mailman," explained Lars.

After they finished their grapefruit soufflé, Julia said, "I've been thinking more about what we talked about on the sand dune today. I've decided that I want to be a spiritual consultant of some kind. I had a vision of what my business card should look like." She removed some colorful ink pens from her purse and drew a bright sunshine mandala on a napkin.

Lars looked at the mandala. "I have some graphic design computer software, maybe we can crank out a few cards," he said. Within hours, they created numerous business cards to Julia's specifications.

"These look wonderful!" beamed Julia. To celebrate, they lied down and did snow angels amidst the layers of mail that lined the floor. Soon they were in each other's arms, rolling around and kissing amongst the letters, postcards and catalog supplements.

An hour later, Lars was sleeping on the floor next to Julia when he started to dream.....*a bartender poured drinks in a dark, murky bar, a palpable feeling of dread in the air. The bartender had no face, just gray gauze fabric covering his head. Lars, in his postal uniform with a full mailbag, walked up to the bar. "What will it be, sir?" asked the bartender.*

"I'd like some absinthe, heavy on the wormwood," said Lars.

"We have no absinthe, only grapefruit juice," replied the bartender, placing brightly colored plastic cartons on the bar. "We have Florida Fun, California Jubilee and Sunshine Splash."

Lars turned around and looked at the other people in the bar. They were hunched over in postal uniforms, drinking grapefruit juice from festive plastic cups adorned with happy sunshine designs. Like the bartender, the customers' faces were invisible, all covered with masks of gray gauze fabric that had straw insertions enabling them to suck up the juice. "Grapefruit juice is a good source of Vitamin C," recommended one of the bar's patrons helpfully, holding a plastic cup in the air.

Lars noticed a man at the end of the bar whose face was not covered by gray cloth but instead was obscured by half a grapefruit that he was stuffing into his maw, slurping and sucking noises mixing with the dripping pulp. Staring at the grapefruit that was seemingly attached to the man's face, Lars approached the end of the bar and stopped a few feet away. The man removed the grapefruit from his face, revealing himself as the Postmaster General. "Get back to your route, Lars," said the Postmaster General while pointing at Lars' stuffed mailbag. Ferrets suddenly appeared on the barroom floor, gravitating toward Lars' legs, biting his black-socked ankles with sharp teeth, *herding him out of the bar……*Lars awoke from the dream, Julia still asleep and breathing peacefully in his arms.

As days went by, the weather cleared up and more people were on the beach, soaking up the sunshine and playing in the waves. Julia had been reading the book 'The Sunlight-Filled Life' and her mind was floating on waves of New Age thought, visions of chakras and energy vibrations crowding out the data and programming structure that had filled her mind a few days before. While walking along the beach, Julia looked at people around her, seeing a family get into an argument over how best to set up a beach umbrella. She also noticed a man squeeze the last white glops of sunscreen out of a tube onto his pale flesh, then angrily throw the tube into the sea. While staring at the empty tube of sunscreen floating in the ocean, Julia had an epiphany, deciding that what she wanted to add a dimension of light-filled spirituality to the lives of beachgoers. She approached the family that was arguing about whether to close or open the beach umbrella. "Fear is the energy which contracts and closes, love is the energy that opens and expands," counseled Julia.

"Mind your own business," said the father, struggling with the umbrella in the wind.

"So you feel that the choice of love would be to open the umbrella?" the mother asked Julia.

"Yes, open your soul to the energy of the universe," said Julia.

The couple's child asked, "Won't opening the umbrella block out the energy from the sun?" but by then Julia had already moved down the beach toward the man who had thrown the sunscreen tube into the water.

"I won't go into my objections to your littering," began Julia, "but don't you think that you're projecting your own spiritual disquiet onto that tube of sunscreen?"

"What? Who are you?" asked the man.

"I'm Julia," she said, giving the man her new business card, which had no words on it, only a sunshine mandala. "You can contact me for further spiritual consultations by just putting the energy out into the universe." She walked away as he stared at the card.

Over the next few days, Julia wandered along the beach, offering more advice. "You have to truly see and feel the sorrow of the world. From that sorrow will come compassion, and from that compassion will come love," she said to a child who was crying because her ice cream had fallen off of its cone.

Most of Julia's philosophical suggestions were met with bewilderment by beachgoers. "We've noticed you walking along the beach, dispensing psychological and spiritual bromides, what's your deal anyway?" asked a couple wearing matching swimsuits.

"I don't have a deal, it's just something that I need to do," replied Julia while clutching a 'crescent moon pentacle' amulet.

A number of people, though, were enthusiastic. "I like what you have to say, can we get together to talk again?" asked a woman after Julia had expounded upon the need to get in tune with one's inner light.

"Yes, tomorrow at sunrise, touch the midmost tree by that picnic bench and you will find me," answered Julia mysteriously. She handed the woman her mandala business card. Through word of mouth on the beach, Julia managed to accumulate an affluent clientele, many of whom were receptive and willing to pay substantial amounts of money for the philosophical messages she provided on the barren stretches of sun-soaked sand.

On a bright Saturday morning, Julia woke up and leisurely ate breakfast: half a grapefruit, whole wheat toast and tea. She opened the window and savored the sea air. Julia gathered her business cards into a bag and walked out onto the beach. Waving to Lars, who was farther down the beach finding valuable coins with his detector, Julia thought about how money was now finding her when she stopped pursuing it and did what she loved, as instructed by the book, 'The Sunlight-Filled Life'. Stopping to stare at the waves on the beach, Julia realized that she had an imminent appointment to lead mantra chanting in a sea cave with a group of spiritual seekers. She had no conventional electronic or ink-stained calendar but instead relied upon intuitions about when the next appointment should be, based on the patterns of clouds in the sky or the textures of oceanic shrubbery growing amidst rocks and tide pools. Her instinctual scheduling was very accurate, and she arrived punctually for every meeting.

On her way to the sea cave, Julia encountered a man with a long white beard and weathered skin. He was dressed in a caftan robe and seemed to be speaking in sign language to the sun, his hands and fingers bending in crooked angles toward the solar rays. In Julia's mind, he resembled some sort of Maharishi, and she picked up on his spiritual vibrations instantly. "Namaste," she said in a tentative greeting as the man turned toward her.

"I've seen you walking on the beach, and I know your type," he said while eyeing Julia's mystically-themed necklace, pendant and anklet. "You think that appropriating material replicas from ancient cultural traditions will somehow bring happiness and spiritual knowledge, but your supposed spirituality is nothing but materialism and faux Eastern mystical posing."

Julia was taken aback but then replied, "I'm doing what helps keep me on a spiritual path, which, if I may add, is different for everybody. What should I be doing, making hand signals at the sun?"

"There can be just as much mind-blowing spirituality in your daily routine as there is in supposed cosmic mysticism," responded the man.

"So I guess you're not an ascetic sage," said Julia disappointedly.

"No, actually I'm an information technology professional trying to enjoy my weekend," said the man, his fingers casting crooked shadows on the sand. Julia gave him her mandala business card.

As Julia had more spiritual discussions along Grapefruit Beach, Don called a meeting of the programming staff at InfoGrab. "As most of you know, Julia quit, but I don't see it as a big loss, we're looking for people who fit into our culture," began Don.

"She was actually a really good programmer, with certain skills and unique abilities that just needed to be understood by management," piped up Alex, annoyed that his friend had been driven out of the company.

"No, she just didn't fit in," said Don and Cindy dismissively. Ed scowled at Alex and scribbled something on a notepad.

"Now we have a few openings on the team, with the departures of Morris, Roland and Julia, so I encourage you to keep your eyes open for any potential replacements. If you refer somebody that's subsequently hired, there may be a bonus in it for you," said Don.

"Yummers!" gushed Cindy. Alex thought about Bill Pleck, who had been dragged out of TechniSel raving and screaming, wrapped in Ethernet cables. Perhaps he would fit in here.

Alex's smartphone rang when he returned to his cubicle. The voice on the other end of the line, much to Alex's surprise, was that of his old college roommate Omar. "Hey Alex, long time no hear!" Omar filled Alex in on what had been going on in his life. Alex was not surprised to hear that Omar had founded a lucrative tech startup company, gotten married and had two children. Omar had also bought a house in the suburban neighborhood where Alex had grown up. "It's an optimal location near my company, and all the factors just added up for us to move there," declared Omar.

"Hey, well I'm going to be coming up there on vacation in a few days, we should get together," said Alex, and they made plans to meet.

Alex traveled north for vacation, visiting family and friends. Late on a Saturday afternoon, he drove a few short blocks from his parents' house to Omar's house, a large McMansion with kids' toys on the front lawn. Alex noticed how luxurious the house looked, compared to the wild decaying vine-covered apartment building he lived in at the beach. He rang the doorbell and

Omar's wife Rena answered the door. "You must be Alex, welcome! Come on in!"

"You have a beautiful house," said Alex.

"Thank you. Omar is in his office, just finishing up some work." Rena led Alex down the hallway.

"Alex! Hey man, how you doing? I'll be right with you," said Omar, in the midst of a conference call. "We need to have the contract with that vendor signed by Tuesday!" said Omar impatiently into his smartphone while beckoning for Alex to sit down in an office chair on the other side of the desk. Eventually, the call completed, and they repaired out to the back deck with a couple of beers. "Yeah, the job does take up a lot of my time, but I love it," said Omar. He checked his smartphone for text messages. "It's something I belong to, it's part of my identity. I thrive on tech innovation. Rena also works full-time. She's a software engineer at a tech company. How about you, Alex, what have you been up to all these years?" Alex filled Omar in on his life at the beach and his various computer jobs.

"The corporate goals never really turned me on, but I always try to do the job and not let down the people I work with," said Alex.

"Still the same old Alex, just doing enough to get by," smiled Omar, confirming in his mind his impression of his college friend as being both a competent hardheaded pragmatist and a flake.

Omar's phone rang. "Excuse me, Alex, I have to take this call." Omar's two young children wandered into the backyard and Alex played soccer with them on the extensive lawn while Omar spoke with his executive team on the phone. "Sorry about that, Alex, we have a big production rollout going on, so things are a bit hectic. I see you've met the kids." Omar's smartphone beeped again and he looked at it. "Rena just texted me from the kitchen. Dinner will be ready in 5 minutes." Omar and Alex got up from the redwood deck chairs. "My parents are here, this will be a good chance for you to meet the whole family," said Omar.

Sitting down at the dining table, Alex was introduced to Omar's parents Vaughn and Beryl. "So you're the computer expert, are you? I've been having some problems with my PC, maybe you could take a look at it," said Vaughn.

"Alex has been telling me about his interest in driftwood, seaweed and kelp," said Omar with a smile.

"The what?" asked Beryl.

"I've gotten into making sculptures out of seaweed, driftwood and kelp, I guess it's kind of a hobby," said Alex.

"A hobby?" inquired Beryl dubiously.

"These days, my artistic endeavors amount to turning the focus knob on an old television set that we have," said Vaughn, adding, "I went through a phase, wanting to be a painter before I grew up and accepted my real-world responsibilities."

"I had a lot of fun playing soccer outside on the lawn with the kids, they're great!" said Alex, changing the subject.

"Do you have any children, Alex?" asked Beryl hopefully.

"No," said Alex.

"How about marriage, do you have a woman in your life?" persisted Beryl.

"Uh no, I'm single," said Alex.

"Oh really, well good for you," said Beryl distantly.

Omar's smartphone rang and he said, "Uh-oh, there's a big emergency with our production rollout, I'll be right back."

At the same time, the children started crying loudly from another room. "Excuse me, I'd better see what's going on in there," said Rena, getting up to check on the kids.

"So you live at the beach where you can play with driftwood, seaweed and kelp," began Vaughn as he poured some more wine. "Don't you think it's time that you grew up and accepted real-world responsibilities?"

"I am meeting my responsibilities," said Alex.

"Which are what? Making sure that enough kelp has washed up on the beach?"

"What's wrong with doing something different and following your dreams?" asked Alex.

"Your 'dreams' should be the wholehearted devotion to a career and raising a family! We wanted grandchildren, and Omar has provided them. A childbearing marriage between a man and woman is the only acceptable choice," insisted Vaughn, feeling anchored in his confidence of knowing how things should be for everybody.

"Alex, you should be having children," said Beryl, a trace of pity in her voice.

"Why do you both say there's only one way to be?" said Alex, building a wall up in his mind as the conversation progressed, knowing that they would never understand his point of view, he being the one who's 'different', they being 'normal' and very invested in it. "Not everybody has the same idea of what success is," he added.

"So are you what we're supposed to call a 'Free Spirit'?" asked Beryl after taking a long gulp of wine.

"I don't know, I'm just a person living my life," said Alex, not wanting to be labeled.

"Someday you'll learn that this is the way life is: you get married, you have children and you work at a job you don't like in order to meet your responsibilities," insisted Vaughn.

Omar returned to the dining table. "Sorry, I got caught up in another crisis with the company," he said. "Did I miss anything?"

"We were just telling Alex that there comes a time in which we must all grow up," said Vaughn.

Rena came back to the dining room. "The kids are quiet for now, though I think they'll be acting up again soon," she said tiredly. Her phone alerted her to a text message, and she read it. "Sorry guys, I'm on-call at work, and a problem has come up with the weekend inventory processing. I'll need to deal with it."

Omar's smartphone then beeped with a text message from his company. "Oh man, excuse me for a minute, another major crisis with our production rollout," he said.

"We'll check on the kids," said Vaughn and Beryl, getting up from the dining table.

Alex finished his dessert while Omar and Rena tapped away at their smartphones. "Sorry Alex, this work issue is taking longer than I thought," whispered Omar.

"It's getting late anyway, I should probably get going," said Alex.

The children started screaming again from the other room. Omar and Rena paused their texting and gave Alex hugs goodbye. "It was great seeing you, Alex," said Omar.

"Thanks for dinner. It was good seeing you, too, let's stay in touch," said Alex, as Vaughn, Beryl and the children yelled chaotically at each other in the other room.

After Alex left, the work problems slowed down and the children were tucked in. Vaughn and Beryl said goodnight and drove home. Omar and Rena went to bed after that. "I like your friend Alex, he seems pretty cool," said Rena.

"Yeah but he's never quite fit into anything, always searching. Maybe he'll find what he's looking for someday. I'm glad we have what we have," said Omar. They hugged, kissed and went to sleep, Omar dozing off into a dream…*he was walking along a whitish rock outcrop beside the ocean. A few white stucco houses sat on the hills above. Omar was wearing a simple robe and there was no noise except for the waves gently breaking on the rocks. He took a deep breath of ocean air and looked along the white outcrop. It seemed like a blank slate open for expansion into anything, not cluttered by electronic overload. The thought of it filled him with unexpected calming happiness.*

Then suddenly he felt a jolt and was inside a prison cell. Leaping threateningly at him was a grapefruit attached by a chain to one of the prison cell's walls. The thrusting citrus was yanked back by the chain. A guard passed by and inserted grapefruit pieces into Omar's cell through a slot in the door. Omar picked them up and chewed upon them ravenously as the grapefruit on the chain continued to lunge at him. Through window bars, he looked out and viewed the whitish rock outcrop on which he had just been wandering. In the ocean below the outcrop, Omar saw his friend Alex riding a cheap plastic boogie board, catching wave after wave but never crashing into the rocks. Omar recalled the one time he'd been boogie boarding, when he'd tried to do a selfie, inadvertently dropping his phone into the water. "Hey Alex, why are you out there on that boogie board!?" called Omar from the prison cell.

"I'm living in the moment!" shouted Alex, waving upwards from the ocean.

Omar turned and looked down the whitish rock outcrop, seeing a small figure on the edge of the ocean, holding a smartphone to her ear. It was Rena. "Rena!! It's me, Omar!" he yelled from the prison cell, but she did not hear him.

Omar turned back toward the inside of the prison cell, where the previously lunging grapefruit now sat still, attached to its chain. Omar snatched the grapefruit and cut it open with a knife, finding a swirl of wires and circuits within. He held the grapefruit to his ear, hearing static. Omar looked again at Rena, far down the whitish rock outcrop, still out of reach, on a different communication wavelength. Slowly her voice emerged from the grapefruit's circuitry, amidst the static. "Omar, why do you prefer to escape into your work instead of being with us, your family?"

"That's not true, Rena!" he lied.

"Omar, you don't even know me, and if you took the time to find out how I really feel, you wouldn't like it," said Rena's voice.

"We hate you, daddy!" echoed the voices of Omar's children in the background.

"Rena!" shouted Omar, but there was no response, only static and the noise of the surf. Shaken, Omar looked down the whitish rock outcrop, where Rena still held a phone to her ear. Turning towards the inside of the cell, Omar saw it filling to the brim with electronic equipment: computers, modems, monitors and keyboards. Feeling relieved, Omar was able to sign on to a computer and check his email, getting caught up on his company's production rollout status.

When Alex got back to Grapefruit Beach, he found Julia wandering along the sand with a bubble-blowing kit, creating thin spheres of liquid-enclosed air that flew off into the sky. "How was your vacation?" she asked.

Alex went on to tell her about seeing his parents, and his visit with Omar. "Compared to Omar, I feel like I'm doing nothing with my life. He has so many things going on," Alex said glumly.

"Well, everybody has a different reason for being on this planet," said Julia, blowing more bubbles and releasing them into the air. "Are you happy with your life the way it is?" she asked.

"Actually I am, it's just some other people who seem to have a problem with it," said Alex, referring to his recent conversation with Vaughn and Beryl.

"Then it's their problem, they're just projecting their own fears onto you. Well-meaning people will often offer up advice as to how you should live, all based on their ideas of how things should be so that they will feel comfortable," Julia said as the bubbles bounced around on some moss-covered rocks.

"Alex, we've hired a new programmer," announced Cindy upon Alex's return to work from vacation. She and Alex walked down the office aisle, stopping at a cubicle. "Alex, this is Blake, the new member of our programming team."

"Hi Blake, how's it going?" said Alex.

"IT'S A PLEASURE TO MEET YOU, ALEX!" boomed Blake. He crushed Alex's fingers as they shook hands.

"Blake, I like your enthusiasm!" declared Cindy, "Alex, I want you to get Blake acclimated to our work culture and be available to answer any questions he might have."

"Okay Cindy," said Alex.

Don walked down the cubicle aisle, saying, "I see the new member of our team is here."

"Yes Don, I've just been getting Blake settled in here," said Cindy.

"Blake, I like the cut of your jib. I think you'll fit in better here than those malcontents Julia, Roland and Morris did," said Don. The other manager Ed greeted Blake and stared intently at him, seeing the new employee's soul as a moldable piece of clay.

Cindy reminded Alex and Blake, "Hey guys, don't forget our mandatory team-bonding lunch today!"

Soon Cindy, Alex, Blake and a couple of other programmers were in Cindy's Toyota subcompact, headed to a restaurant for lunch. "I stayed up all night debugging a program, but I had Mr. Uni with me, so it was okay!" said Cindy while reaching down to the floorboard to pick up and wave around the little pink stuffed animal that she often kept within close proximity. "I couldn't figure out what the coding problem was, and Mr. Uni was getting annoyed," said Cindy, frowning at the pink unicorn.

Turning a corner, they drove by a woman singing and dancing on the sidewalk. The woman looked a lot like Dove, and Alex did a double-take, examining the woman's face, seeing a close resemblance, though he could see it wasn't Dove. "HA-HA! LOOK AT THAT WEIRDO!" shouted Blake.

"Hee-hee, she looks like a head case!" agreed Cindy while stroking Mr. Uni on the head.

"She looks like somebody I used to know," said Alex, staring out the window and thinking about Dove, wondering how she was doing.

Cindy returned to her story. "Finally, I figured out that I hadn't allocated enough space for the output files in my program, so I fixed the problem, and Mr. Uni was relieved! HA-HA-HA!" She veered the car hazardously in traffic as Alex stared out the window, feeling lonelier in this car full of people than he would have felt by himself.

Over the next few weeks, Alex was struck by how little work Blake did, despite his professional and efficient appearance. As part of Blake's training, Alex sat down with him and shared some information about sequential and keyed data retrieval methods, though Blake was more interested in searching through an online catalog of InfoGrab coffee mugs, t-shirts and hats that he wanted to get, merchandise which would further corporatize his appearance and personality. Cindy walked over to where the two were talking. "How's the database extraction code going, guys?" she asked.

"JUST SWIMMINGLY!" roared Blake.

"You're dressed very well today, Blake," said Cindy, approving of Blake's business attire. "Alex, I hope you'll follow Blake's lead and try to look more professional." She scowled at Alex's somewhat disheveled beach bum appearance. Cindy went on to inform them that there would be a big new project requiring extensive overtime hours. "It will be a great opportunity for team bonding, we'll be here day and night working on our programs!" she gushed, thinking of the programming team as a surrogate family.

"I'M READY TO TAKE ON ANY NEW PROJECT!" boomed Blake, tightening the double Windsor knot of his tie. Alex looked at Blake and saw a hard shiny aggressive nightmare dressed for success.

"That's great Blake!" squealed Cindy.

Don walked down the aisle, ready to share a joke. "Hey Blake, have you heard the one about these two fag rump-rangers walking down the street?"

"HA-HA-HA!" laughed Blake heartily as Alex rolled his eyes.

"I try to see the complexity and depth in people, but with this person, there doesn't seem to be anything else there," said Alex to Julia as they walked along the beach during the weekend, discussing the new employee Blake. "It's like he's a loud empty husk, a blank shell laughing vapidly at Don's homophobic jokes."

"He sounds like a perfect fit there, I'm glad I don't work for that company anymore," said Julia as they moved along the sand toward some tide pools, finding a grapefruit lodged amongst some small starfish. "Though to be fair, you don't really know him in depth. We find it easier to label and categorize people because we only see the surface appearance. Blake could actually be a deep, thoughtful, questioning, complex person, with a complicated history based on all sorts of adversity and hardship."

"Yeah maybe," said Alex doubtfully while looking at some rockweed and sea lettuce splayed out near a clump of ice plant.

The next day, Cindy, Alex and Blake worked through the morning and afternoon on the programming project as it rained outside. After completing a difficult section of code, Alex went to the lunchroom, where he saw Blake putting popcorn into the microwave. "So what do you like to do on your free time, Blake?" asked Alex, attempting to engage him in conversation. Alex looked into Blake's eyes and saw nothing but a cold empty gleam.

"MY SOLE INTEREST IS THE FURTHERANCE OF INFOGRAB'S GOALS!" bellowed Blake, pulling the popcorn out of the microwave and stalking out of the room.

Cindy passed by the lunch room and looked in approvingly. "Now that's the kind of attitude we need around here! Alex, you could learn something from Blake's example!" Feeling more and more fed up with his job, Alex soon began working on his resume.

After work that day, Blake drove home in drizzling rain, his hands gripping the steering wheel of his car as he maneuvered through rush hour traffic. The windshield wipers shifted back and forth, squeegeeing the raindrops off of the glass in front of his face. He looked at the self-help books that were spread out on the passenger side of the front seat. Well-known tomes like 'How to Win Friends and Influence People' mingled on the car seat's vinyl upholstery with 'The Sunlight-Filled Life' and other newer books. Fired from his previous job, divorced from his wife, drowning in a sea of financial debt consisting largely of alimony and child support, Blake's day-to-day consciousness was filled with anger and resentment that he tried to modulate with pleasant, empowering thoughts from 'The Sunlight-Filled Life'. Pulling into the parking lot of the complex where he was renting a small anonymous furniture-less apartment, Blake scowled at the red 'Engine Check' light that started blinking on his dashboard. He got out of the car with the self-help books stacked in his arms, rain pelting down on the paperback covers. A book that described self-empowering pathways to healthy relationships fell into a mud puddle. "Goddammit," muttered Blake. He bent over to pick up the book, its yellow-flowered cover immersed in sludge. Arriving at his apartment door, Blake thought about the people at his new job. The managers and team lead, i.e. Don, Ed and Cindy, would be easy to manipulate with a ready smile, a loud assertive voice, a clean pressed suit and a seeming willingness to do work. He didn't know what to make of his co-worker Alex, who just quietly did a lot of work and would occasionally space out to stare at those pictures of driftwood, seaweed and kelp on his cubicle wall. Alex seemed disengaged, and Blake decided he would use that to his advantage.

The next day it rained again, and Blake sat in his cubicle, reading 'The Sunlight-Filled Life' instead of working on his program. "You can be free of the 'usual' reality where people just recite expected lines based on their fears, the fears of others, and societal conventions that are questionable or began in ways that don't make sense. Just follow your inner sunlight!" urged a passage. Blake quickly became bored with the reading and switched to a book on Marketing. As Alex passed by, Blake announced from his cubicle, "YOU NEED TO AGGRESSIVELY MARKET YOURSELF MORE, ALEX!"

“Yeah Blake, maybe the beach has mellowed me out too much,” replied Alex as he went back to his desk to work on some report generation code.

As the afternoon shifted into the evening, Alex’s phone rang. “Alex, this is Julia. Lars and I are going to go out tonight and experience the rain. If the clouds clear up, there’s going to be a full moon, come join us!” Alex looked around the office area. Cindy was rapidly typing in data, her fingers dancing along the keyboard. Blake was busy with social media on his smartphone.

Alex got up and walked over to Cindy’s desk. “Cindy, I have an emergency and I need to leave now,” said Alex.

“You’re leaving?” asked a startled Cindy.

“Yes, something has come up, but my main program is done, the system testing was just completed.”

“All right, we’ll see you tomorrow,” said Cindy with a frown.

Alex left the building and crossed the near-empty parking lot to his car, his senses opening up to the cool misty evening rain. He drove back to Grapefruit Beach, where he found Julia and Lars on a sand dune, dancing in the rain. Though hobbled on crutches, Lars was turning and swaying to a hypnotic inner beat. “Alex! Imbibe this nectar of the cosmos,” intoned Julia, offering Alex a small dusty bottle filled with a greenish maroon liquid. “We have a concoction of natural roots, fungi and herbs!” Alex took a sip from the glass vessel and felt his mind fly off into the sky, soaring amidst the rain-filled clouds. For the rest of the night, he, Julia and Lars danced and frolicked in the rain, laying their souls bare to the full moon, which came out after the clouds cleared. Alex would remember the night for the rest of his life and resolved to have more experiences like that.

"Alex, I hope your 'emergency' was resolved last night," said Cindy when Alex got in to work the next morning.

"Yes Cindy, it was, thanks," said Alex.

"I hope you won't be making a habit of taking off like that," she admonished, displeased that her team had been disbanded for an evening.

"YES, IT MUST BE NICE TO TAKE TIME OFF LIKE THAT," boomed Blake from his cubicle while reading the book, 'Win At All Costs'. Alex sat down at his desk, put on his earphones, and got started on some database updates.

The minutes ticked by, Blake went home, and Alex kept working as the day yielded to night. By midnight, Cindy got up to leave, saying, "I'll be back at 3 a.m.!" Alex kept working, and then fell asleep at his desk, where he floated off into a dream...*he was in a deserted town square filled with portentous orange and yellow light. Surrounding the town square were small buildings that cast black shadows on the sun-baked ground. A couple of grapefruits rolled around in the dust. Alex wandered through the square and then turned down a side street, discovering that it was filled with armless Venus de Milo statues. Backing away from the sculptures of amputation, Alex heard a flapping sound and saw a large foreboding shadow cover the ground. He looked up at the sky, seeing a massive yellow bird diving straight toward him, its black eyes zeroing in on its prey. "Millions would kill for your job!" squawked the bird as its talons tore at Alex's arm. "Why can't you fit in and be a real team player?!" demanded the bird with a piercing shriek.*

"I am! I complete my required assignments!" yelled Alex, fighting against the bird's snapping beak.

"That's not enough!" screamed the bird, its talons digging deeply into Alex's arm. "We want your soul as well!" The bird's claws pulled again and ripped Alex's right arm off, the detached limb falling into the dirt. Alex wrestled himself away from the bird and staggered through a door of one of the adjacent buildings, but not before the big yellow bird ripped off his other arm, leaving him armless like the Venus de Milo statues he'd seen on the side street.

Inside the building, Alex slammed the door shut with his foot and turned around, finding himself in a cocktail party, strobe lights flashing and music playing loudly. All of the guests had bird heads, and as Alex looked at each one, it seemed as if he was viewing them through an odd camera lens, the bird heads appearing in strange angles and extreme close-ups. A waiter approached him with a tray of champagne flutes filled with grapefruit juice, and bowls of niblets. Alex, still armless, took a glass with his teeth and declined the bowl of corn niblets. Immediately a group of party guests approached him, the men in tuxedoes and the women in cocktail dresses. They all had bright yellow bird heads and were clutching bowls of corn. "Why are you not eating any niblets? You're refusing to fit in!" squawked one of the bird heads, its long sharp beak filling Alex's vision at a crooked close-up angle. "You need to follow the etiquette of our social circle! Hold your champagne glass in your right hand in a certain way, while your left hand holds your hors d'oeuvre dish, which should be filled with niblets!"

"But my arms have been torn off!" shouted Alex. The group of party guests then started screeching, cawing and clucking, descending upon him. Alex fought back, head-butting and kicking, knocking a number of them to the ground before their sheer numbers subdued him. Held down to the floor, Alex struggled as the bird-headed party guests poured bowls of niblets on his armless torso and began pecking at him, their busy squawks drowning out the sound of his screams...a shrill ringing phone woke up Alex at his desk. It was 2 a.m. and he was in a cold sweat. "Alex this is Cindy! Just letting you know that I'm on my way in to review your programming code. I'll bring cookies and fruit punch, it'll be fun!"

A few days later, Alex was walking down a hallway at InfoGrab when he heard "Pssst…" A door leading into a conference room was slightly ajar, and Alex looked inside, seeing a number of software engineers sitting around a table. He recognized some of them. "Quick, close the door!" whispered a programmer named Camryn who seemed to be leading the group. Alex closed the door and sat down. "Alex, we've formed a rebel group that's going to nail InfoGrab to the wall! We've organized and we're going to hold InfoGrab accountable for their managerial abuses!" said Camryn.

"This group already has a track record of success. We demanded a Casual Friday and they caved in!" said one of the software engineers at the table.

"Alex, we know that you're not one of the enemies and that you could be a key piece within our puzzle! We're going to meet on Saturday and Sunday to discuss our strategy! We'd expect you to commit a certain amount of time to this cause!" said Camryn.

Alex had plans that weekend to hike in the mountains with Julia and some other friends. His way of rebelling was to disentangle himself from the goings-on of the company as much as possible. "Yes, okay, though it looks like I might be busy this weekend," he said.

"Okay, we'll be in touch again soon with an assignment schedule!" whispered Camryn urgently, as they all got up and left the conference room.

The next morning, the management team met for weekly status reports to the division vice president Glynis. After a number of managers gave their reports, Glynis said, "Ed, what do you have for us this week?"

"Well Glynis, as you know, we've been monitoring the activities of this so-called 'rebel group' in the programming division."

"Yes, for the last few weeks they've been struggling for a 'Casual Friday', on which they can wear Hawaiian shirts to work, and we finally granted it to them. It made them feel like they're winning battles," smirked Glynis.

“Well, we’ve recorded their latest conversation, thanks to a microphone that we hid in a potted plant,” said Ed, going on to play the recording of the rebel group’s conversation.

After listening to the recording, the management team identified a number of the participants, though incompletely. “We need to know the names of the other people in that room!” demanded Glynis, her hard porcelain-like face and platinum hair shining under the room’s lighting. “I want you to squeeze the known conspirators and get them to talk!” she ordered, her eyebrows arching dramatically.

“Yes, we know this programmer Alex was in on that conversation, so we’ll work on him,” said Ed.

“Okay good, thank you, everybody, meeting adjourned,” said Glynis. “Oh, Ed, could you stay a minute?” After the other managers left, Ed moved forward towards Glynis in his ergonomically-compliant conference room chair, his slacks inches away from her nylon stockings. “You’re my little pit bull, aren’t you, Ed,” said Glynis knowingly while tapping his head with a riding crop.

“Yes, Glynis, anything for you,” said Ed, longing with lust for this woman and her power. He licked the black boots covering Glynis’ feet, enjoying the sordidness of it all.

Glynis felt pleased that she’d gained an understanding of Ed’s need to express an inner darkness. It was important to assess the motivations of one’s subordinates. She removed a whip from a black leather briefcase and commenced to striking Ed repeatedly with the lash. “You like this, don’t you Ed!” ordered Glynis, the whip stinging swift and true.

“Yes, Glynis!” screamed Ed, feeling a release of inner tensions.

“Alex, management has decided to assign you a new project that will increase your participation!” chirped Cindy the next day. “Don and I will fill you in on the details!” They walked down the hallway to Don’s office.

“Come on in!” said Don, beckoning for them to have a seat. Ed was in the corner of the room, staring intently at Alex as Don spoke. “Now Alex, I’ve realized that though you’ve been with the company for a while, we really haven’t gotten to know you.

You've met all the work requirements here, but we really don't know what makes you tick."

"Just tell them what they want to hear," thought Alex to himself, going on to describe some of his recent accomplishments and his work in getting Blake up to speed. "I'm really just trying to help the company reach its goals," Alex concluded.

"Good man," said Don, giving Alex a verbal pat on the head, "but we really need to know that you're onboard with the company's objectives."

"Now what's this interest you have in driftwood, seaweed and kelp?" asked Ed, referring to the beach pictures Alex had tacked to the corkboard walls of his cubicle, "you do realize, don't you, that we prefer our employees' interests to be golf and childrearing?"

"I think Morris would have had pictures of nude men in his cubicle if he could have gotten away with it," grumbled Don, in reference to the gay former employee. "The bottom line, Alex, is that we need you to have a real passion for this line of work as Cindy and Blake do." Alex nodded, imagining himself on the beach in a cool sea mist, looking for kelp. "To expand our department's exposure, we'd like you to participate in a social media video we're creating. It will be a good way to increase your visibility," continued Don as he pulled a box out from under his desk. Bright yellow feathers fluttered out of the box as Don opened the lid. "Alex, we'd like you to wear this bird outfit and extol the virtues of working at InfoGrab." Don extracted the avian fabric ensemble from its container.

"It's like Big Bird from Sesame Street, but with more of a technological edge," said Ed, pointing out a user interface located beneath the wings.

Bright yellow feathers fell off of the costume onto the floor. "Some glue will get those feathers back into place," said Don. "Now Alex, while you're wearing this bird outfit in the video, you'll be singing the InfoGrab song. Cindy, would you please?"

Beaming a delighted smile, a chill of pride running down her spine, Cindy got up and intoned the anthem of allegiance to InfoGrab. Upon completion of the song, she began evangelizing about team camaraderie and the importance of their mission. "We're a part of something momentous, Alex, and I think you and the others should be very proud of the work we're doing!" Alex looked at her. What he felt 'a part of' was getting paid and trying to maintain a semblance of work-life balance, as he'd seen enough of Cindy in action to develop a cynical attitude toward this sort of proselytizing. She'd grabbed credit and placed blame with abandon, anything to maintain her reputation as a superstar within the company. Alex believed that the chief beneficiaries of his hard work would be Cindy and management, but he tried not to dwell on these disagreeable thoughts.

"Alex, if you successfully complete this project, we will know that you truly fit in. It will brand your identity for the world to see, as being a member of our team," said Don. Alex's mind was filled with his recent dream of the big yellow bird tearing off his limbs.

"Now Alex, we also know about that meeting you had with the so-called 'rebel group' a couple of days ago, we had a microphone hidden in a potted plant. However, you'll be back in our good graces if you provide us a list of all the programmers who participated in that little insurrection," said Ed, the hypnotic abstract design on his polyester shirt swirling violently.

Feeling InfoGrab's diseased talons clawing at his soul, Alex finally said, "I'm not going to do any of this, you people are out of your minds." He got up from his chair and walked out of the office.

As Alex left the building, he saw Don, Ed and Cindy hovering around Blake's cubicle. "YES, I'LL WEAR THE BIRD OUTFIT!" enthused Blake.

Alex spent the next day walking along Grapefruit Beach. The surf was crashing and water sprayed high on the rocks. He waved to Lars, who was up on a sand dune with his metal detector, finding more doubloons. Farther down the beach, he saw Julia chanting with a group of other spiritual seekers. No longer with InfoGrab, Alex thought about what to do next with his life. He noticed more grapefruit accumulating along the sand.

Part 2: The Grapefruit

Julia left the apartment building and walked outside on a foggy Tuesday morning. She crossed through the adjacent garden of rhododendron, azaleas, poppies, hibiscus, butterflies and hummingbirds. Parts of the garden were going to seed, with wild new plants sprouting and spreading throughout. Reaching the beach, Julia stepped forward, her toes enjoying the grains of sand. She noticed some grapefruit plants starting to take root amongst the ice plant and shrubs that heartily occupied the sandy reaches of the beach. Julia walked down to the shoreline, where a grapefruit washed up from the frothy waves, rolling through the sand near her feet. "Looks like breakfast has arrived, maybe Alex would like to share this with me," she said to herself while picking up the grapefruit and placing it into a bag.

When Julia arrived at Alex's apartment, he was on the phone with Camryn, the leader of the rebel programmer group at InfoGrab. Alex waved to Julia and she sat down at the kitchen table with the bag of grapefruit.

"Are you free to talk?" urgently whispered Camryn on the phone line.

"Yes Camryn, I'm no longer with the company," said Alex.

"So I've heard. They've replaced you with a programmer named Bill Pleck, who's just been released from the madhouse. He seems very pliable," reported Camryn.

"Yes, I know Bill," said Alex, thinking that Bill Pleck must have made great strides in his rehabilitation.

"Alex, we are bringing InfoGrab management to its knees! We demanded a 'Workers Appreciation Day', on which we'd spend 10 minutes every other Thursday eating cake, and after significant recalcitrance, they relented!" crowed Camryn triumphantly. Alex looked over at Julia, who sat by expectantly with her bag of grapefruit. "Now Alex, our group has former InfoGrab employees as well, keeping up the good fight, and we'd like you to be one of them! Our group has scheduled a number of nightly strategy sessions, starting tonight!"

"Well Camryn, I'm just looking to move on with my life, and put InfoGrab behind me," said Alex as he headed out the door with Julia.

"Yes Alex, I can understand that, but what we're doing is important, and we still feel that with some commitment, you can be an important part of the team!" Alex and Julia walked out to the beach with the grapefruit as Camryn kept talking on the line until there was static and the phone disconnected.

On the beach, Alex and Julia saw their neighbor, Lars, scanning the sand with his metal detector and finding nothing. "I may be going back to work at the post office tomorrow, the beach is no longer yielding valuable coins," said Lars, a bit glum despite his characteristically optimistic nature. He swept the electronic instrument over the sand again, but the sensor made no beeps of discovery.

"Yes, I think I'll need to return to work as well, and get another programming job. My clientele for psychological and spiritual counseling on the beach is drying up, and I need to pay the bills," said Julia while clutching the bag of grapefruit. She and Alex asked Lars if he'd like to join them for breakfast, but he declined, still sanguine about the possibility that he might find more doubloons.

Julia and Alex walked over to a spot near a moss-covered rock and began consuming the juicy pulp of the large, round, yellow citrus fruit. "Yeah, I might be going back into I.T. as well," said Alex as he dug a spoon into a grapefruit. Since leaving his job, he'd been feeling adrift like a piece of driftwood, part of him still needing the structure of information technology, and he had no illusions that sculptures of driftwood, seaweed and kelp would generate even a minimum amount of income. "Maybe I'll get back into computer operations, the kind of job I first had when I got into I.T. It paid less, but at least it didn't seem as if they were trying to possess my soul," he said.

"Yes, it might give you a little more space to find what's true for you, and your path to the truth may run through a combination of driftwood, seaweed, kelp and computer data," said Julia. She finished her half of the grapefruit and threw away the peel.

"So what about you, Julia, what will your path be?"

"I don't know, I like the idea of seeing myself as a blank slate open for possibility, there's a lot of freedom in that. I'll probably do enough I.T. to pay the bills, but also still counsel people on the beach, and who knows what else." Some waves churned and crashed on a large rock nearby.

"Yeah that sounds cool," said Alex. He eyed a conglomeration of kelp that was materializing with the incoming tide. "Whatever you do, I guess you won't be worried about 'fitting in'."

"No, 'fitting in' is overrated, I'd rather just be me," said Julia. She adjusted her 'chakra interchange amethyst' anklet.

"I once heard somebody say, 'Instead of being the best in the world at what you do, be the only one in the world who does what you do.' I've always liked that," said Alex, becoming increasingly interested in the growing pyramid of kelp nearby.

"Yes, everybody has something unique to add to the world. If you can find what you love to do, and get some time doing that, then you're one of the lucky ones in this life, no matter what anyone else says," said Julia. She got up from the sand with the bag of grapefruit peels. "I don't know, maybe it's not about fitting into a job, but rather finding a job that fits into your life. Anyway, I'm going to go meditate on my career plan."

"Okay Julia, see you later," said Alex while moving toward the stack of kelp.

After her meditation, Julia returned to the apartment building, where she saw a piece of paper taped to the front door. It read, 'Tenants: As of next month, the rent will increase by 300%. Signed, The Management.' "What the hell is this?!" she blurted. Looking down the beach, she saw Alex still investigating the mound of kelp. "Hey Alex, come here, you've got to see this!"

Alex came over and Julia pointed to the piece of paper. "What the @#$%!" Alex exclaimed.

"Let's go see the manager," said Julia as she tore the notice off of the door. They walked down the building's dank hallway to Lunski's apartment and knocked on the door.

“Hey guys, I see you got the notice,” said Lunski as Julia held the piece of paper up to his face. Alex looked around Lunski’s room, noticing a nude woman sitting at a table, hunched over a chessboard, deep in thought as she contemplated her next move. The woman did not acknowledge their presence. “The building’s ownership is raising the rent 300%, I have no say in the matter,” said Lunski.

“So who is this ‘ownership’ anyway?” demanded Julia.

“I’ve never met them,” said Lunski, “but all of their communications are signed, ‘The Grapefruit’.”

“The Grapefruit?” asked Alex. The nude woman at the chessboard muttered something about Duchamp and overturned the board, plastic bishops and pawns falling on the floor. She lit a cigarette and stared out the window.

“Yes, I don’t know who they are, I’ve only dealt with their intermediaries,” said Lunski as a piece of paper slid under his front door. Lunski picked up the paper, on which were written the words,

‘Dear People,
Meet us on the beach.
Signed,
The Grapefruit’.

He opened the door and looked down the hallway, but there was nobody there. The nude woman put the pieces back on the chessboard, said “Check,” and then stalked out of the room.

Alex, Julia and Lunski walked outside, where numerous grapefruit were strewn along the walkway. The citrus orbs seemed to shift slightly as if turning their attention to the three humans entering their vicinity. Feeling uneasy, Alex, Julia and Lunski moved on to the sand, where they saw Lars, still hunting for coins with his metal detector. Nobody else was on the beach. They showed him the piece of paper indicating the rent increase. "Have you heard that the grapefruit might own the building?" asked Alex.

"What?!" replied Lars as dozens of grapefruit began appearing in the waves, washing up onto the shore. Once on the beach, the group of grapefruit rolled forward on their own accord and then stopped to stack themselves, slowly forming a wall about 10 yards away from the apartment tenants. As the four people looked at the growing barrier of citrus, they felt a strange aura on the foggy beach, an irreal landscape of sand and frothing waves forming in their minds.

From the wall of grapefruit, a single grapefruit dropped off and rolled to the fore, identifying itself as the 'head grapefruit'. It seemed to be vibrating with electricity and had a little mouth that voiced its words in a sonorous tone. "Hello people," said the head grapefruit, "I suppose you're wondering why we've asked you here."

"Yes, that thought had crossed our minds," said Julia.

"Do you really own the apartment building?" asked Lunski.

"Yes, we do Mr. Lunski, and as the apartment manager, you've been a useful pawn in our strategy, but we've decided to escalate our plan of aggression against you humans, a plan that only begins with the raising of your rent," said the head grapefruit while squirting bitter juice in Lunski's direction.

"What's this all about?!" demanded Julia.

The head grapefruit rolled toward her. "We've been observing you humans for quite some time, perhaps you've noticed us appearing in your day-to-day activities, as well as your dreams."

"Yes, especially our dreams," said Alex.

"As the gateway to the subconscious root of your motivations, dreams are the best way to get at you," said the head grapefruit.

"Why are you trying to get at us?" asked Alex.

"Why does anybody invade or attack? It can be self-defense, a thirst for power, or one of many reasons. In our case, we don't owe you an explanation because we are nature, and nature is an inextricable force, just doing what it is compelled to do. Does an avalanche or a tidal wave explain itself before wreaking havoc on innocent defenseless populations? No. Does poison ivy expound upon its motives? No."

"You've heard of a bad seed? Well we're a bad crop!" interjected another grapefruit.

The head grapefruit continued, "We've seen your human social dynamics, your pursuits of self-realization, your concerns about fitting in, your attempts to find work that is fulfilling, your little games of one-upmanship, and it all amounts to nothing. It will not take precedence over the force of nature moving forward inexorably!" The head grapefruit began bouncing up and down with excitement.

"Isn't human interaction another form of nature? Are you saying that one form of nature is truer than another?" asked Lars. The head grapefruit ignored his question.

"Is this nature's revenge for man's environmental pollution of the planet?" asked Alex.

"Well a few of us have that gripe, such as these two," said the head grapefruit, rolling toward a couple of greenish citrus spheres on the left side of the pile, "but that's not our primary motivation."

"What about our rent?!" demanded Julia.

"We're way past the point of discussing rent, Julia," said the head grapefruit, spinning sinisterly. "You see, we are reaching you through the mind's back door, the black root, the dream world."

The fog grew thicker as the four people looked around, feeling the intuition of an encroaching bizarre dreamscape, images beginning to emerge in the fog. The humans looked up toward the main highway, where another wall of grapefruit was forming, blocking the road. A truck labeled 'Have a Nice Day Charities' crashed into the wall of grapefruit and exploded in a ball of flame. By the water, two otters sat at a table playing chess, studying various strategies as the foaming surf swirled around the table's four wooden legs. On a sand dune stood a man wearing a black tuxedo, his head consisting of nothing but butterflies. The man held a revolver in his right hand and was shooting bullets into the center of a sunflower growing out of his left arm. Down the beach, standing starkly in the fog, was a solitary wooden doorframe with a closed door. "Perhaps you should follow us," said the head grapefruit, rolling through the sand toward the door.

Alex, Julia and Lars followed the grapefruit, but Lunski hesitated, looking toward the otters playing chess. "Lunski, where are you going?" called Julia as Lunski walked toward the otters.

"Only the otters understand me," muttered Lunski. When he arrived at the otters' chessboard, he moved a black knight to queen's bishop 4, and declared, "Checkmate!"

"Fine move, Mr. Lunski," said the otters, impressed, "come join us for a swim."

"The ocean and chess, two things I love, it's all coming together," said Lunski. He picked up the otters' chess set and walked into the waves, joined quickly by the two semiaquatic mammals. The three of them swam past the waves, emerging in still, calm water, where they set up the floating chessboard. Lunski and the otters played chess as they drifted out to sea, disappearing over the horizon.

"#39, it looks like we'll need a new apartment manager," said the head grapefruit to another citrus sphere.

"I'll get right on it, sir," said Grapefruit #39 eagerly, rolling away from the group back to the apartment building.

"Now the rest of you, let's go through this door," said the head grapefruit while rotating rapidly toward the solitary doorframe, knocking the closed door open.

Alex, Julia and Lars followed the grapefruit through the doorway, which led into a beach landscape filled with computer equipment. Large and small data systems were ensconced in the sand amidst aquatic life. Starfish and sand crabs sat atop laser printers, keyboards and monitor screens. Routers and modems were situated in tide pools, the hardware's green, yellow and red informational lights blinking efficiently. "What reality are we in now?" asked Julia.

"A melding of the conscious and unconscious into your true world, an alternative reality of which many concurrently exist," replied the grapefruit, adding, "we are your reality, just think of us as the power of the unknown and the mysterious."

"I'm thinking of you as annoying," said Lars while swinging his crutch at the head grapefruit. The crutch arced through the grapefruit with no impact, as if the citrus didn't materially exist.

"Don't you see, Lars, you can't do any physical harm to us, we exist in your mind, where things cut deeper than anything overtly physically violent." A grapefruit vine began twisting around Lars' wooden crutch. "Lars, to make our point, we are going to help you evolve from a purely physical form into an unencumbered spiritual essence, free of corporeal limitations." A group of ferrets sped across the beach, aiming toward Lars' leg. Lars recognized the ferrets from his earlier turbulent experiences as a mailman, and they acted quickly, chewing at his right leg, completely tearing it off, rendering him an amputee. "I believe the ferrets have been appearing in your dreams too, they have been useful allies in our mission," said the head grapefruit as the ferrets masticated on Lars' other leg, making him a double amputee.

Lars' crutches were still useful in this situation, and he maneuvered himself over to a stunned Julia. "I have hope. Even when things seem at their worst, I believe that something good is going to turn up. I have a blind optimism for no discernible rational reason," he said, giving Julia one final kiss before the ferrets would resume their work, removing the final remnants of his physical manifestation, freeing him into a purely spiritual existence. But suddenly after he sanguinely said those words, the onslaught of the ferrets receded, and they faded back into the depths of the sand dunes.

The head grapefruit stirred angrily and consulted with the others, as some lemons rolled over a sand dune, approaching the vicinity. "When life gives you lemons, make lemonade," offered the lemons cheerily. The group of grapefruit quickly responded en masse, rolling forward to crush the lemons in a puddle of bitter juice.

As Julia helped Lars situate himself on his crutches, Alex stared further down the beach at the computer hardware lurking in the sand and windblown weeds. He saw people from his past information technology career suddenly appear.

Julia then looked down the beach too, seeing a man in a polyester retro disco shirt building a sand castle dungeon. She recognized him instantly as Ed, the manager who had driven her out of InfoGrab via an insanely hostile infiltration of her dreams. Attempting one more time to provide psychological and spiritual counseling on the beach, Julia approached the abusive Ed, his hands clawing at the sand. She thought about what she had read in 'The Sunlight-Filled Life'. "Did you know that most of an abuser's abuse is connected to their own fears of intimacy?" probed Julia as Ed turned his head up to look at her. "I can sense that you've been hurt in this life, well 'hurt' people hurt people," continued Julia. She looked into Ed's eyes, peering under his psychological mask to see fear and craven motivations, along with a trace of humanity. "Somehow, I see something decent within you. At some point you were a good, kind person," insisted Julia as Ed assessed her with hard black eyes.

"No, I'm just a sadist," said Ed. He grabbed at her face with a pinching malevolence, his hope of being anything different having long since disintegrated. Julia pulled away.

The head grapefruit said, "Ed has been a useful vehicle for our anti-human purposes, but his glimmers of self-importance are proving to be his undoing and he's becoming redundant." Numerous grapefruit rolled forward, covering Ed in a smothering pile. He screamed as the tangy fruit orbs suffocated him, utilizing pulp and rind to obstruct his breathing mechanisms. Repulsed yet relieved, Julia viewed Ed's final moments of struggle for oxygen. The citrus spheres moved around on the sand after pushing Ed's inert body down into the sand, the incoming waves washing over it. "It's just how we roll," said the head grapefruit happily.

Alex saw two office cubicles on the beach near a wave-crashed rock. Inside one cubicle was Pam, Alex's supervisor at TechniSel, and in the adjacent cubicle was Morris, the programmer who had been recently fired by InfoGrab. They were typing busily on their keyboards in the sea air as large waves splashed the cubicle walls, leaving pools of whitewater foam swirling around their business shoe-clad feet. After a particularly large wave struck the cubicle walls, Pam and Morris emerged from their desks, dripping in saltwater. They approached a water cooler lurking near the cubicles and drank small paper cups of water while discussing office intrigue. The conversation turned toward their feeling of being outliers in the corporate world, and their desire to start their own software company. "The unconscious reality is where our hope is able to manifest and take root," said Pam. Alex was able to see how, in their own ways, Pam and Morris never felt like they fit in either, so maybe they weren't so different after all, especially since they all now had a common enemy, i.e. the grapefruit. "Everyone doesn't fit in, some are just able to hide it better," noted Pam.

"You will not be able to start your own software company. Your business plan is flawed, it's going to fail," mocked the head grapefruit. "We have a belief that it won't fail, and we're going to try anyway," said Morris as he walked into the fog with Pam, kicking a grapefruit along the sand. The citrus spheres stewed in their bitter juices, unable to act in the face of hope.

"So, the humans are being brought together by hope, isn't that sweet," said the head grapefruit acidly, as from behind a row of sand-covered magnetic tapes and spinning tape drives emerged Lloyd, 'The Void' from Alex's earlier days as a computer operator with the construction company. The Void was dressed in his customary blue button-down shirt that covered his formidable paunch.

"Hello Alex, how are you doing here in the world of the dark subconscious?" asked The Void while holding magnetic data tapes in one hand and mysterious occult amulets in the other.

"I don't know, Lloyd, I'm still trying to figure that out," said Alex.

Julia gazed at the mysterious otherness emitted by The Void, entranced by his metaphysical aura and projection of ethereal wisdom. The group of grapefruit watched, knowing that Lloyd was their tool, dissolving positive life forces into null, bleak non-manifestations of nothingness, the antithesis of hope. "There are beautiful philosophical traditions associated with The Void,"

Lloyd said softly to Julia, impressed by her cosmic jewelry. "Julia, we are at the entry point to the limitless whirlpool of emptiness. Take my hand, and we'll find ultimate freedom." In Julia's mind, this was what she had been in search of, all of her mandalas, pendants and talismans adding up to this moment, The Answer. Julia moved her hand forward, about to take Lloyd's grip when she turned and looked at Lars, amputated on his crutches and filled with pathetic hope. Not able to act otherwise, Julia reached out and took Lars' hand, helping him with his crutches. Hissing, Lloyd disappeared into the foggy mist.

"Follow your soul, Alex!" called Julia, as she and Lars hobbled down Grapefruit Beach, fading away in the distance.

"Well Alex, that just leaves you and us," said the head grapefruit, stirring angrily on the sand, upset that Julia had not followed The Void into nothingness. Alex looked at the strands of seaweed washing up on the sand. "You love the driftwood, seaweed and kelp, don't you Alex? We just cannot understand that," said the head grapefruit.

"For me, it symbolizes hope and potential that anything can happen. I suppose that source of hope varies for each person," said Alex.

"Well, in the dream world anything **can** happen. It's where people can relate in a whole new way, on the unconscious plain," said the head grapefruit. It rolled around on the sand and then continued. "Alex, we like that you think independently and question things, quietly rebelling in your own way."

Alex thought about some I.T. managers he'd had in the past, who'd attempted to manipulate him with similar flattery. "Maybe my hope lies in the questioning itself," he said.

In response, the citrus spheres stirred around in the sand and then stacked themselves, reforming their wall. "Like your managers, we just want to get at your enigmatic core, and find out what makes you tick," said the head grapefruit. Alex heard large wings flapping in the sky and looked up, seeing the big yellow bird from his dreams, circling with talons extended.

"Perhaps humans are unfathomable and you'll never get that answer, no matter how hard you try," said Alex.

"We'll see," said the head grapefruit, and Alex suddenly felt himself veering into.... *a diner on a hazy Wednesday morning, eating a breakfast of eggs, bacon, toast and grapefruit after having worked the night shift at a computer company. "Can I get you a refill on that coffee, honey?" asked a waitress smoking a cigarette with a long, dangling ash.*

"Thanks," said Alex, holding up his coffee cup and pushing his spoon into the grapefruit. When he dug the cutlery into the citrus, he discovered an ocean roaring inside of the grapefruit's core, waves splashing against the pulp and rind. The grapefruit then rolled off of the plate and plopped onto the diner's linoleum floor. It rotated out the front door, where it morphed into a glowing ball of light and energy. The ball sped through adjacent

avenues, absorbing and accumulating experiences from Alex's life. Alex chased after the glowing ball of light as it maneuvered through streets and frontage roads, headed towards the ocean. At the beach, the ball of light absorbed energy from mythical marine creatures draped in seaweed and kelp, sitting on chunks of driftwood.

"Maybe you are a vessel of these aquatic spirits from underwater forests, where the seaweed and kelp lie," opined the diner's waitress, suddenly appearing in the waves, her lit cigarette defiantly sending smoke into the sea air. "Or perhaps the grapefruit represents the dark side of humanity, your shadow self," she mused, adding, "just figure out the glowing globe." The ball of light rolled quickly through the beach sand, lodging itself amongst some rocks. Alex ran toward the rocks, trying to find the ball of light, searching and searching....

...until he suddenly found himself back in front of the barrier of citrus spheres on the beach, unsure of whether this was still a dream or some new form of reality. The waves brought in more seaweed and kelp that twisted around Alex's ankles as he remained in a standoff, his hope fighting off the wall of grapefruit.